Defeating Loneliness

PETER H. BURGESS

authorHOUSE®

AuthorHouse™
1663 Liberty Drive, Suite 200
Bloomington, IN 47403
www.authorhouse.com
Phone: 1-800-839-8640

First published by AuthorHouse 3/24/2008

ISBN: 978-1-4343-6089-2 (sc)
ISBN: 978-1-4343-6253-7 (hc)

Library of Congress Control Number: 2008900219

Printed in the United States of America
Bloomington, Indiana

This book is printed on acid-free paper.

The Scripture portions are taken from the Authorized King James Version of the Bible.

THIS BOOK IS DEDICATED

TO
ALMIGHTY GOD

DR. PETER H. BURGESS

AMANUENSIS

TABLE OF CONTENTS

Introduction

This treatise has been designed to provide material to assist one who is suffering from isolation and subsequent sequestering in their life's journey. Multitudes are facing loneliness and depression due to their mistreatment by individuals, society, and most unfortunately, by well meaning spiritual establishments. Using all means of written materials gathered, as well as personal interviews and observations, we will present pertinent information to help extricate those in conflict. There is an unseen enemy in our midst which is to be exposed and there is a means of escape for those incarcerated by the socio-spiritual environment they encounter which will be revealed in the pages to follow.

Our current day society is all but oblivious to the malady which is being addressed in this study. We must face the facts and take appropriate action as spiritual leaders to help eradicate this serious condition. This subject is long overdue and we do an injustice to the body of Christ when we ignore this decided enemy of our souls. Unfortunately, there has been miniscule research in this field of study and we must draw upon all resources, personal interviews and the genuine experience of this author in order to present substantial evidence as to the causes and treatments of this serious condition. Our personal involvement and participation should create facts as opposed to theories.

Individuals from all walks of life have been incorporated into this research, i.e., men, women, youth, together with lay people, and theologians. No areas have been excluded from study and all the information is authentic and carefully recorded to insure the credibility of this impassioned endeavor. There are definitely some controversial issues introduced in these pages, but again, being honest and forthright is of extreme importance. As the old adage states, "The truth hurts." For genuine healing to occur one may well have to face some hurting in the process.

In order for the sequestered to be emancipated from their circumstances, there needs to be a valid solution employed on their behalf. It is, therefore, incumbent upon those who counsel to understand the tactics of our common enemy and how to overcome the evil one. This is the reason for this treatise. There are no limits to what may be accomplished by dedicated folk who are educated to the devices of Lucifer. Theologically, all those dedicated to godly principles should recognize our failure in the past and may the favor of God rest on all who desire to become a friend to the friendless in the future.

Every aspect of our biblical lives will be exercised when we gather our thoughts and innermost spirit in this exposé of utmost importance in our day. There is no question that this topic has not become front page fare for most Christians. The theme is replete with multitudes of avenues for one to traverse in their Christian experience. Information has been compiled from seminary libraries, the internet, news media, and multiple volumes gathered over the years by this author. Scholars from yesteryear to this current day have all been included in this dissertation. In spite of the lack of extensive information on this theme, the research has unearthed most valuable and conclusive data and has been coupled with extensive personal observation and experience. The study of this provocative topic shall provide invaluable wisdom and should prompt those involved in the humanities to become indefatigable in their pursuits.

PROLOGUE

Pain is our best friend. Many may respond that with such a friend, there is no need for an enemy. And yet, if we try to dismiss pain as an annoying messenger, it could well lead to even more devastating pain. Such neglect may result in serious illness or total incapacitation. Pain needs to be acknowledged and addressed.

Where does it hurt? For those of us who are experiencing on-going trauma as a result of some sort of isolation, the pain can be inexplicable. It becomes all but impossible to capture in words this human emotional nightmare. In utter desperation we search for relief. Some of us seek out a counselor, or an empathic companion, while others of us may visit a psychologist or even a psychiatrist. And then, still others may regrettably resort to snuffing out the very lives God has given them in complete desperation of their plight.

If you have, or are experiencing such a scenario, you are a prime candidate for a spectacular encounter. It may prove to become even more painful than what you have encountered up to this point. However, you may find relief in a certain solace which will be addressed as you examine the forth coming pages.

All humanity is created for the sole purpose of glorifying their Creator and enjoying Him in blessed fellowship. Whenever we fail in this God provided relationship we discover ourselves washed up on the shore of frustration. We attempt to pull ourselves together, looking for something or someone to fill the vacancy in our life; a life left devoid of any real meaning. Ultimately, we conclude that there is definitely a missing piece in our life's pilgrimage.

The subject which has been long neglected and needs to be explored is that of unadulterated loneliness. We have become socio-spiritually sequestered. We have become so engulfed in this ploy by our common enemy that we have failed to comprehend the real cause of our entanglement. Again, all who may have become disoriented in the maze will want to examine why things continue to become so complex in their lives. There is a way out of this serious situation which may be unveiled in the scriptures and through gifted and devout people who once sat where you now sit. Therefore, let us proceed prayerfully and expectantly in what may prove to free you of your emptiness, desperation, isolation, and yes, your loneliness itself.

Oddly, at first glance, the subject known to us as that of loneliness does not seem to have been covered in God's love letter to us. How preposterous, as loneliness seems to plague most of us at one time or another. Sooner or later those of us who have become isolated due to life's circumstances may reach the threshold of what we can bear. The results can be agonizing and overwhelming.

Even though our Master has not seemed to confront this matter head-on, we catch glimpses of loneliness in the lives of biblical characters and ultimately even in the life of Christ. We wonder how John's traumatic loneliness on the isle of Patmos may have affected him psychologically. And yet, he managed to pen a discourse which is found in a book that tops the best seller list! Yes indeed, my friend, keep in mind that it does become lonely at the top!

Judah is described in Lamentations, the first chapter, verse two, as one who "wept sore in the night and her tears are on her cheeks: among all her lovers she has no one to comfort her: all her friends have dealt treacherously with her, they have become her enemies."

Again, the sweet Psalmist of Israel pours out his heart in distress over a special friend who left him bereft, as recorded in the fifty-fifth Psalm. David's friend has taken him "to the cleaners," having left him as a wounded Samaritan on the highway of life. Talk about real loneliness. This was the ultimate.

Can you identify with these biblical characters? If the answer is "yes", then you are likely to succeed in dealing openly with your deepest trials, just as your predecessors did. You need only to yield to the Holy Spirit of God and allow those with godly expertise to guide you to victory. There is hope for all who are entangled and sequestered by the enemy.

As a result of the times in which we now find ourselves we may be tempted to engage in substance abuse, sexual promiscuity, isolationism, or any number of self-destructive behaviors. Some of us may even resort to thoughts of suicide to relieve our suffering. It is here that we can meet our Creator in a fashion which we have not previously experienced or pondered. Up until this period in life there has been no real, lasting significance in the journey. It's like a dream. This becomes the moment God has been waiting for. We are divinely loved beyond our greatest expectations.

In writing on the awesome theme of loneliness, John Eldridge draws our thoughts to such, "Loneliness might be the hardest cross we bear. Why else would we have come up with solitary confinement as a form of punishment? We are relational to the core."[1]

Keep in mind that we are created in the very image of God and thus He understands and is equipped to assist us. He alone is acquainted with our grief, sorrow and solitude. Listen! God employs the pain of loneliness to draw us into a genuine and meaningful worship that we cannot fully appreciate prior to this experience. Such is a type of relationship which is not of man's orchestration, and therefore, not subject to the manipulation and exploitation evident in far too many human relationships.

A pertinent case in point is supplied by the journeyers to Emmaus. Christ indicates His intention to proceed on His solitary way when they arrive at those travelers' abode. Our Lord, Himself, implies His being lonely and desirous of human fellowship and personal attention. We get lonely. Did it ever occur to us that He has a deep longing for closeness, as well? It is definitely not a one-way street. His ultimate goal for all of His divine creation is that of genuine worship. Revisiting John at Patmos reveals that his ultimate sequestering led to the apex in what we ponder as God's acceptable form of worship. When the gross darkness of lonesomeness overtakes you, it is then that God can get you into that which He defines as worship. The process is exceedingly painful but the results are priceless.

Keeping all of this in mind, biblical counselors are often beset by counselees who are in search of advice for a multi-faceted set of obstacles. These obstacles may be broken down into various compartments. Those counselees may be diagnosed with depression of various sorts; inferiority, insecurity, neurosis, schizophrenia, etc., when in fact, the basic need may well stem from a breakdown in their relationship with the Creator who put them together in the first place. When a time piece is malfunctioning you need not venture to give it to a psychiatrist for an adjustment. God, alone, will cause us to get upset in order to set us aright. We come with our empty container in desperation to be filled. The ultimate solution in bringing us into a healthy relationship and answering our very phobia is to be made complete in our Maker. Our desperation is solved in His completeness. Therefore: " Be still and know that I am God." Let Him take control.

A Christian psychologist has brought to our attention that "the highest dream we could ever dream, the wish that if granted would make us happier than any other blessing, is to know God, to actually experience Him. The problem is that we don't believe this idea is true. We assent to it in our heads. But we don't feel it in our hearts."[2]

Scripture is replete with accounts of saints that find themselves alone with no road map, no guide, no light in sight. What they did discover was that there is a special compass out there and often times the Lord will allow solitude in order for the seeker to get His message. We definitely do not appreciate what is transpiring in our respective lives but our Lord knows the way through the unpleasant wilderness before us. Dear God, it's lonely! Yes, but we learn it is for our growth and development. In other words, there is more to the Christian life than escaping the abandonment of eternal retribution. It is more than some form of playing church, i.e., wood, hay, stubble. There is a life of holiness and a devotion to the Almighty which may not be a giddily blissful life but one which is to be holy and joyful in our dedicated walk with Him.

"People everywhere are afraid of loneliness. It is feared as an enemy of body and soul. It is a powerful force that drives homosexuals and lesbians to despair. Those involved in that life claim they experience a kind of loneliness that only few can comprehend. Often, it drives them to suicide. Addicts, alcoholics and prostitutes live with overwhelming loneliness every waking hour. But all the time, it is God at work, wooing them back to Himself."[3]

As we delve into this socio-spiritual sequestered treatise, in the sociological, spiritual removal from others, we must not forget that God can use such an experience to draw us from this world to a special revelation of Himself. Loneliness is an emotion apart from the classic examples of love, hate, fear, anger, etc. We may well have become remiss in our recognition and comprehension of this seldom addressed phenomenon.

One must not become ignorant in searching for the source of a malady or the root cause of an emotional response to any given situation. This is especially true of the subject at hand. Loneliness may be the result of a personal infliction, an attack from the enemy, or from God's own intervention. In any case, God will use whatever source for His glory and for the recipient's edification. No matter what happens to us, it must never create bitterness within but must direct us to an ultimate God-likeness. It is with such a stance that we are open to learn at the feet of the Master. We may not know His plan in our being left destitute, sequestered, and all by ourselves in a cold environment.

However, in all of this, it is believed by this author that He is there in our utter despair. In that lengthy passage in Psalm one hundred nineteen, verse one hundred fifty one, there is a magnificent revelation. While writing this verbose message the psalmist stops suddenly and observes that in his presence is the Lord, Himself: "You are near, O Lord."

This special observation comes at the end of the many topics mentioned throughout the psalm. When we come to the end of ourselves we discover He is all we need to dispel the gloom. In our continuing examination of this all-engulfing monster, which leaves us nonplussed, we shall discover how to overcome this socio-spiritual sequestered manifestation.

There are many facets to the subject at hand, but for the sake of a somewhat clearer comprehension, it may be that we can separate loneliness into three basic components.

Many choose loneliness in the same manner as does a hypochondriac in search of an illusive illness. Others will discover themselves engulfed in this state due to the loss of someone or something. Then, there are those who become sequestered as a result of the action of friends, family or some other relationship. This may come out of a business experience or even pleasure, at times. At any rate, we are left to ferret out the basic underlying reason for the condition in our desire to help people extricate themselves. Upon discovery of this latent phenomenon, we may set out to be of assistance to our fellowman. Unfortunately, many of our religious institutions are not equipped to come to the aid of the destitute socially or spiritually.

"One of the greatest faults of intellectual Protestantism is that it has tended to stifle emotion. The Sunday services have more resembled a lecture series than a worship service."[4]

It is with this gathering storm of isolation, desperation and consequent loneliness that we engage in such a study. It will not be answered by a mere study but through the very heartbeat of the Almighty working in the hearts of dedicated people. We will submit the facts but ultimately one must catch a vision and get into the fray. Believers are to get out from the four walls of the sanctuary into the hurting masses in our communities. It is never too late to get involved in the call of God which has been overlooked by indifference all too long. As an old baseball devotee has put it: "it ain't over til it's over."

And the battle has just begun.

CHAPTER ONE

Detached from Society

It is difficult to convey the horror and indescribable desperation that accompanies loneliness. How can the internal anguish of abandonment be expressed in words? It is the cry of a mourning dove in the depths of the soul. Only those who personally experience such a trauma are able to comprehend the full impact and implications.

> "One of the heaviest feelings in a time of bereavement is the feeling of loneliness. After sharing a significant part of our emotional and physical life with another person, we get used to having them with us. We depend on their conversation, their support, and all the interactions that we shared. When taken out of our lives it creates a huge void."[1]

On March 13, 2006, my dear wife entered a long term care facility as a result of dreaded Alzheimer's. The day she left me she looked at me with saddened eyes to report that she had no friends. It was a true confession. Somehow, my friends had become her friends. She was a most kind and caring person in every manner and was appreciated by many people. And yet, she did not cultivate her own friendships. When counseling others my admonition is for the counselee to build personal friendships separate from mutual friendships they may share with their spouses. Loneliness can be dispelled by a caring soul, a true confidant, who makes conversation by phone or in person.

Today the house, which used to be a home, is empty and quiet and, yes, lonely. The consolation is in that it means that I can spend more time alone with the Lord. This is most unconventional for a man who, since birth, has always been with another person. A feeling of detachment prevails in spite of the fellowship I enjoy with my Master. A sweet little black lady aware of my discomfort said, " You are not alone. The Lord is with you and that is a real blessing." The retort was, "Yes, but God doesn't wear a skirt!"

Wasn't it God who told us that it is not good for man to be alone? And who knows better than He? And yet, God in His wisdom uses *our pain* for *our gain* in our walk with Him.

We listen to His comforting voice in spite of the rejection we are feeling. For oddly enough, even though a loved one may be removed from our lives through illness and not by their own volition, feelings of rejection may still overtake our thoughts.

It is then that we need to recall what transpired when our Lord was rejected, as recorded in Isaiah 53. Christ knows the pain that comes with rejection. He understands our depression. He is acquainted with the hurt that we feel, a hurt that cannot be expressed or measured. It is in dealing with this detachment that we must recall what God is doing in our respective lives; He is wooing us by His Spirit into a divine closeness.

> "When the heat is on and confusion mounts, some believers go through a horrendous spiritual crisis. They 'lose God.' Doubt rises up to obscure His presence and disillusionment settles into despair. The greatest frustration is knowing that He created the entire universe by simply speaking it into existence, and He has all power and all understanding. He could rescue. He could heal. He could save. But why won't He do it? This sense of abandonment is a terrible

experience for someone whose entire being is rooted in the Christian ethic. Satan then drops by for a little visit and whispers, 'He is not there! You are alone!'"[2]

We are prone, both as believers and non-believers, to believe that if all goes well we are being blessed. Don't rock the boat. Avoid black cats. Don't walk under open ladders. Cross your fingers. These hold credence for many of us but such is not in the mind of God. Our Lord's half brother went so far as to admonish us to count it all joy when falling into divers temptations. We, however, are determined to avoid the very "obstacles" that God is employing to shower upon us His greatest blessings. Even Balaam's ass recognized a road block that went undetected by man. Animals are, often, more in tune with the God of creation than we humans.

> "Do you ever sense creation's restlessness? Do you hear groaning in the cold night wind? Do you feel the forest's loneliness , the ocean's agitation? Do you hear longing in the cries of whales? Do you see blood and pain in the eyes of wild animals, or the mixture of pleasure and pain in the eyes of your pets? Despite vestiges of beauty and joy, something on this earth is terribly wrong. Not only God's creatures but even inanimate objects seem to feel it."[3]

In all of this, our lesson for all posterity is that we must never allow ourselves to become betrayed by our feelings. We stand not on feeling but on truth. We must hold on securely to God provided fact, even when emotions would persuade us to believe the contrary. When we are bereft, lonely, and alone, it must not be considered a curse of the Almighty. We must keep before us the eternal truth that God, alone, is in control. It is not Satan who is in control. It is not our so-called friends who are calling the shots.

When we are all by ourselves we must learn to lean on the Lover of our souls, recalling that He longs for our fellowship as well as our worship. Remember, He, too, was rejected. He longs for a special time with His own. We were made in His image. He desires intimacy even as we do.

There may be those in some theological circles who would question if Jesus Christ ever became lonely for human affection. There are implications throughout the gospels that suggest He did. Jesus certainly desired fellowship with His disciples and enjoyed communing with His followers. We, too, long for fellowship. Sadly, our modern day houses of worship do not possess the warmness we experienced from them in yesteryear.

> "Satan's best tools of destruction are not from outside the church, they are within the church. A church will never die from the immorality in Hollywood or the corruption in Washington. But it will die from corrosion within - from those who bear the name of Jesus but have never met Him, and from those who have religion, but no relationship."[4]

Having served Christ as a minister of the gospel for over half a century, it would be safe to relate some personal observations. The greatest majority of churches in our time do not address the needs of the widows, the lonely, nor the general heartbeat of society.

As long as we carry our Bibles, place our money in the offering, and do what seems to be religious, we think we have pleased God. We may know little or nothing about the widow who is admonished by the pastor to give her tithe from her meager social security check but who is never visited by him or any other church members. If they were to visit her, they might discover that her home is in disrepair and meals scarce because of lack of funds. There is a church that I heard about that spent over thirty five thousand dollars for advertisement with fireworks. I submit that God is not pleased with our way of playing church, with little or no regard in our hearts for a hurting humanity.

We read in periodicals that there is a decline in church attendance in the year 2007. What is even worse is the reasons reported as to why this deplorable condition prevails.

"Many members are vulnerable to attrition because of either a nonexistent or immature faith."[5]

The real answer to the quandary is discovered in our Lord's message to the church in Ephesus. The current day church has grown very large but, at the same time, very cold and unfriendly. Recently

I asked a church attendee the duration of her being a part of a local assembly and was told that it was approximately nine years. Next, I asked her how many friends she had acquired over the years and her answer was, "None." This lady is friendly but is never invited to a social event and is extremely lonely. God is not enthralled with our hospitality no matter how much we contribute or how faithful our attendance. When our Lord returns will He find a saving faith on this planet?

> "Eventually there comes a feeling of utter depression and isolation. It is as if God is no longer in His heaven, as if God does not care. It is during these days we are sure that no one else ever grieved as we are grieving."[6]

How is this loneliness dispelled? How do you rid the utter darkness of a room? Does one go about it by removing it by the bucket full? Absurd! Turn on a light and away it goes. We dispel isolation and a spirit of loneliness by the light of the Word, by being a friend to the friendless. Community is absent from our Christian vocabulary.

People become withdrawn and detached because no one seems to care for them. The answer to this social and spiritual sequestering is so complex that we avoid it. The people of God must take cognizance of this travesty lest our enemy engulf them soon and suddenly. We cannot, we must not, allow those whom God has entrusted to us grope in darkness until they end up on medication or until their lives end in death. Throughout this treatise we have become aware and alarmed over a neglected malady, a malady, that if not addressed shall be our undoing. It is my opinion that many of our illnesses stem from an unseen condition, unlike any other faced by counselors. That great monster is none other than that which we are now addressing, namely, rampant social and spiritual sequestering.

> "Elijah wanted to see if God was going to do something miraculous just because he was a prophet. Well, after Elijah cried again, God responded, 'Go your way.' I call this cave experience. You're feeling lonely, forsaken and as if no one cares. It is hard to face your future. You're ready to hang it up but then,

God always shows up but not in the way you expect. He doesn't always heal or do a miracle. Sometimes He just lets you know in a quiet voice, 'I do love you.'"[7]

But do you know what? I really do believe that as His mouth and arms we need to step up and with a loud united voice tell the lonesome that God loves them and so do we and here is a hug from both of us.

To help those who are assisting patients with Alzheimer's, which affects the care provider more than anyone else, several suggestions were provided to the Alzheimer's association. The care providers often find themselves alone in their ministry. For most who fall into this difficult category are often overlooked in deference to the patient. Thus, some helpful suggestions would be to ask those in such a plight how you might assist them. You need not supply your advice as most have plenty of that. Just listen. Be positive and never negative. Call periodically on the lonely provider. Bring a meal that is home-cooked. Offer to visit with the sick relative so that the care provider can go out on business, etc. Suggest going for a walk. Are there any errands you could do for them? But most of all, let them know that they are definitely in your thoughts and prayers. Let them know that you will be there for them during their bouts with desperation and isolation.

Now let us take inventory. Just how many souls do you think will heed such suggestions? We allow so many to travel through this life without being there for them. Loneliness is, without doubt, one of the main, if not the most paramount, cause of depression. This is the precise reason people in our society become detached, lost in a maze. As the prophet questioned over two thousand years ago, "Is it nothing to you, all you that pass by?" We are not on an island by ourselves nor are those who call for our attention. The usual response to our fellow man is that we are not in a position to undertake the responsibility of living by the side of the road and becoming a friend to man.

"'I can't.' These two words usually mean one of three things: 'I won't'; 'I don't understand my resource in Christ'; or 'I don't know how to do what the Bible tells me to do.' 'I can't' signifies rebellion against God."[8]

This statement may not demonstrate your ability to become an astronaut but it does mean that you and I are most likely able to assist those who have lost their navigational system and we have a responsibility to do so.

The world in general has no real genuine concern. However, we who are redeemed have a divine calling to watch out for those who are sequestered and abandoned. God holds each of us responsible and had the church been doing its job we would be residing in a much better land and climate both socially and spiritually.

A case in point. A special friend in Florida became distraught over his missing dog, Gordo. The entire family went on a vigil for a week looking for this mutt. Posters were displayed and neighborhoods were combed in search of Gordo. Their efforts were rewarded when they found their prized little possession before he was hurt or forever lost to them. But the very best reward came in newly acquired friendships with people who were once strangers to them. The mutual labor in the effort to find this little dog had solidified a community. How often do we pass by our neighbors, seldom speaking to them or getting to know them? We are all negligent but we can begin to change our stance and, in doing so, become better citizens. Studies on this theme will serve to verify this thought process.

> "First, loneliness results from deficiencies in a person's social relationships. Second, loneliness is a subjective experience; it is not synonymous with objective social isolation. People can be alone without being lonely, or lonely in a crowd. Third, the experience of loneliness is unpleasant and disturbing."[9]

Upon becoming detached it is often times exceedingly difficult to get back to healthy communication. This is especially true for those who reside alone. Here is where responsive and responsible people intervene. It is commendable when observant souls seek out any and all who find themselves trapped in their loneliness. It has been my experience that all too many are oblivious to people's longing for friendships and dread the minutest involvement. Most of humanity is preoccupied with selfish concerns.

While shopping in a local establishment a voice is heard requiring a response. You reply to that shopper and find that they are not speaking to you, at all; they are, in fact, on a cell phone! Go to a restaurant and you may encounter the same. Walk around the mall and count the number of people who are talking but not to those around them. Welcome to high-tech and low-communication. This same preoccupation has infiltrated our churches. A mega church serves us refreshments in a large and luxurious hall. We sit next to a hurting fellow parishioner. We are so engaged in stuffing ourselves that we manage to utter only vague pleasantries, if we communicate at all. God cannot be pleased with such behavior in the church. If a person attempts to approach leadership with a need they may find us busy catering to the youth, monitoring the progress of the building committee, or appropriating funds. In our self-absorption we become ill prepared to cope with those who need comforting. People are left feeling abandoned and unimportant.

> "A well-known evangelist spent two weeks in bed with pneumonia. Ministerial acquaintances came from a distance, and despite his high fever, spent over an hour in the sick room, exuding oppressive melancholy. They left with the reminder that, if they never met on earth again, they would certainly meet in glory. The evangelist reported, 'I was far sicker when they left than when they came.'"[10]

Oh yes, what a total blessing! If you are not lonesome and nonplussed you shall soon be. We seem to have become experts at keeping needy souls at bay. Multitudes of believers are at their wits end due to untold numbers of Christians that have become calloused to the desperate cries of those being serviced by their so-called support groups. We must ask ourselves if we, in our blindness, have turned our backs on the lonely and the hurting.

Has it ever occurred to us that, for the most part, individuals mitigate their depression by means of utilizing "security blankets"? Have you ever considered the expenditures laid out each year in this country for pets and pet products? We numb the pain of loneliness and detachment by substituting four-legged companions. There is, of course, nothing inherently wrong with this, but it is an indicator of a longing for love and attention. Often times, we need our pet's attention and affection, but only reciprocate that love when it becomes convenient for us. We may enjoy our pets because they demand so little from us. These faithful creatures seem to love us, their masters, regardless of our disregard or neglect. Then, we may allow these substitute companions to roam freely onto neighboring properties where they are not welcomed. We may have been negligent caretakers of these trespassing pets, but if the offended neighbor even *attempts* to express disapproval over our pet's misconduct we become the offended ones. We would rather hear our neighbors chastise our dear old grandparents than hear them complain about our pets.

Thus, we as humans will go to great lengths to satisfy the need for love and closeness. We will cover up our innermost longings for companionship through any means known to us. We were created to be creatures of community and loners are, actually, abnormal.

> "Loneliness has a quality of immediacy and depth, it is a significant experience - one of a few in modern life - in which man communes with himself. And in such communion man may come to grips with his own being. He discovers life, who he is, what he really wants, the meaning of his existence, the true nature of his relation with other. He sees and realizes for the first time truths which have been obscured for a long time. His distortions suddenly become naked and transparent. He perceives himself and others with a clearer, more valid vision and understanding."[11]

We can become detached and bewildered in our journey through this all too brief pilgrimage. As we cry out to God, our perception is that He seems to have gone deaf. The more desperate we become, the more opportunities God has to get our full and undivided attention. God will, at times, allow trials in our lives in order to refocus our attention on Him. God has a unique way of garnering our attention which may involve both instruction and humor. We, however, never appreciate any form of punishment.

With this in mind, I recall a certain humorous illustration. A little girl had just been spanked by her mother and the little girl was irate. "Why, you have just ruined me for life!" she screamed. Backing her bare bottom up to the large bathroom mirror, she summoned her mom to observe what she had discovered... "See what you've done... You've cracked it!"

We, too, can be just as humorous in our responses to our Heavenly Father. When we are corrected we scream bloody murder but He knows we're getting what we need to become mature in Him. But, all the while, there are certain dark periods when we are sure the He has just completely forgotten us. We feel alone and without hope in a foreign land. It seems that this is when, in our longing and in our loneliness, the most opportune occasion arises for us to embrace His unequivocal admonition and ultimate anointing.

> "Metaphysically, each of us is bound to care greatly for others, even though in his moral freedom he may defer such care. He who does not care at all, or he who cares wrongly, whether he is conscious of it or not, suffers the loneliness of privation of the joy of moral care. And he who cares greatly cannot escape the loneliness of unrequited love. Jesus could not share rapport with men who found fake escape from loneliness in iniquitous living."[12]

And the beat goes on. Yes, the heartbeat of God is that man may enjoy Him forevermore and to love others as He has loved us. God will allow you to gain wisdom in your isolation, which by His grace and our perseverance will lead us down a lonesome path into His open arms.

In our pilgrimage we often run amok in our frenzy to avoid losing our relationships. We fear social isolation. We end up like terrified turtles afraid of becoming shell-less. We fear our vulnerability to an onslaught of careless souls in what we once believed to be a harmless little church. So, after some dreadful experiences, we determine we shall remain aloof which, of course, leads to all that we wish to avoid. In our desperation we find ourselves looking for comfort in all the wrong places. We find ourselves headed down a road that leads us away from the Lord rather than to the safe haven that can be found in Him.

Much of our pain in loneliness stems from insensitive comforters. Job certainly does not have a corner on *that* market. As for Job, his friends were clueless to the ills of humanity. Even Zophar could only go "so far" in assisting a lonely friend in his desperate circumstance. A lonely heart may discover solace in the careful pondering of Asaph's seventy-third Psalm. When we get by ourselves in the solitude of the Almighty we comprehend that we may not be so isolated as we once believed. When He calls us into His presence we discover that our basic needs are not met by man or materialism. Just when we think that God isn't doing anything; that is when God is doing something. In essence, we determine that we have become so preoccupied in our desperation to find solace in material things and human wisdom that we overlook the lonely Savior who welcomes our company and in Whom all our needs are met.

Through all of the introspection on the plight of the sequestered, we must take steps to get a clearer picture of where an individual may be in their situation. There are different phases in this emotional journey. Those who are dealing with such difficult matters and wish to walk a pilgrim through their recovery must determine the root cause of their condition. This will take patience and perseverance. Only those who are gifted and those who are compassionate toward their fellowman can reach any measure of success.

> "Chronic loneliness will be evident from a person's long term inability in relating to others. It will often be characterized by an impoverished social system which has endured for years.
>
> Situational loneliness arises from an individual's present set of circumstances. It results from a disruption of the person's social interrelationships. Examples of this are relocation, death of a spouse.
>
> Transient loneliness arises from occasional feelings of isolation and these are universally experienced by most sensitive and psychologically minded individuals."[13]

There are times when the counselor must determine how extensive the seclusion or sequestering has become. The worst situation is that of a chronic or on-going situation. Other cases may not be as complex, but all take much effort, careful study, and prayerful devotion to determine the root cause. There is certainly no substitute for personal experience in any field, but especially in this one. My own experience has given me insight in assisting the lonely individual.

As a biblical counselor, the strategies I have come to appreciate diverge significantly from those applied in secular counseling and are even acutely different than many of the tactics appropriated in Christian counseling.

Most individuals who are afflicted with a form of detachment, isolation, etc. are prime candidates for what may be termed as a type of alcoholics anonymous program.

Lonely souls need a special support system, or better yet, a support person. Effective support givers need to be consecrated workers, Bible-based, and exceedingly gifted and loving. It takes skill to see that the afflicted regain their equilibrium while guarding against creating co-dependency. The role of the support giver is similar to the role of a swimming instructor. The swimming coach's job is to teach their charge to swim, making sure that the student doesn't drown in the process. While doing this, the instructor needs to be very careful to keep his own head above water so that the beginner doesn't submerge him in his own struggle to keep afloat. Initially, the instructor may hold the novice while he kicks his legs and swings his arms, but eventually he must let go. For those overwhelmed in the icy waters of loneliness, caring and dedicated care providers are invaluable. It is beyond our strength, alone, to be successful in such endeavors, however, through consecration and prayer we find that God is greater than the mission in which we are engaged.

Joshua, the high priest, in Zechariah 3:1, was involved in the things of God as he took a stand for Him. Once we are determined to serve Him with our entire being, we may become surrounded by angels as was Joshua. We can then expect Satan to become more vicious. He will cause you to become unsure of yourself and uncertain of your devotion to your Master. As the time of Christ's return grows near, we can expect even more fierce opposition. Yet, we cling to the promise that He who is in us is far greater than he that is in the world. We must keep reminding ourselves that no matter from what quarter the attacks originate, in the final analysis, we become victorious through Him.

God will allow us to go through the flood or the flame to bring us home purified and safe from all foes. In the meantime, Jehovah will employ us to be His partners in assisting all who are desperate or smothered by loneliness. We will love and assist our brothers into the safe haven of Christ.

Whereas we are often protective, if we are dedicated believers, of those who are friendless, it becomes necessary for us to endeavor to build strong relationships with those feeling forsaken. The Scriptures admonish us that in order to have friends we must cultivate friendships. Those who are friendly are more apt to have friends than those who remain aloof. For some, being lonely may be the result of their own doing. It is imperative that the counselor determine if a counselee is creating an unhealthy environment for himself.

> "No man is an island. No man can be a happy hermit. Loneliness is painful. We must have intimate friends. Again, we must assume 100 percent of the responsibility for building friendships. Solomon said that if we want friends, we must go out and be friendly - we have to earn friends. All humans fear rejection - some more than others. Don't expect everyone to like you. You need three intimate friends. Intimacy is what is needed here, not quantity."[14]

Let us examine the real reason for our being cut off from others before we assume nobody likes us and determine that we must resort to isolation. We must make sure that we have exhausted the possibilities of finding and making close friends before accusing others of failing to be friendly with us. We are, often, our own worst enemy. To correct this, we must flee to those open arms of our comforting Shepherd. In the final analysis, only He knows our make-up and, consequently, the solution to our emptiness is in Him.

CHAPTER TWO

Disturbed Due to Sequestering

There is a relatively new word which may not be included in the dictionary you are now using. Because of its rather recent arrival into the English language, most people are unfamiliar with this term and its usage. That word is ALEXITHYMIA. The word, alexithymia, extracted from the Greek language, is best known to psychiatrists and means: "a lack of words to express one's feelings."

This is precisely the deep underlying condition which plagues individuals who are "boxed-in" by some unsolicited or unnecessary sequestering. Before we go any further, it would be advantageous to define the word "sequester" and how it is being used in this discussion. Sequester: "1. To remove, lay aside, separate, set off or apart; separate; segregate 2. To take possession of as security for a debt, claim etc. 3. To take over; confiscate; seize, esp. by authority 4. To withdraw; seclude." [1]

Almost any of the usages described in the above definition may be applicable to the sequestering of individuals as it pertains to our study. The plight of loneliness may eventually cause a sequestering that fits these definitions. Loneliness may cause one to separate from society stunting their social and spiritual growth and development. The end result can be the confiscation of their esteem, their vision, their values and all they hold precious. Unfortunately, this seizing by authority may often be attributed to Satan, the enemy of our souls, whose purpose has always been to steal, kill, and destroy. Being stripped of confidence and purpose, individuals may then withdraw, leaving them totally isolated. However, the possibility should be considered that our Maker may use this sequestering for His eternal purposes. Therefore, we must become introspective in the diagnosis and never lose hope.

To say the very least, the Christian community, for the most part, is ill prepared to address the longings of a lonely society. We have become so engrossed in all the paraphernalia of "churchianity" that we cannot see the trees for the forest. Mega congregations as well as the smaller ones seem clueless when it comes to helping a hurting humanity. Where can we go but to the Lord? In going to Him we learn that what we do unto the very least, we have done unto Him. There are some awakenings in our fellowships as far as relating to, and reaching out to, those who are broken hearted and lonely. But we certainly fall short of what God expects from His Church.

"Being crucified by fellow Christians is one of the deepest pains a child of God will ever know. It can so profoundly affect you that it can mark the end of your life as a practicing Christian. There is no limit to the effect a crucifixion can have on your life. It could possibly leave you lame for the rest of your life."[2]

However, we, who are in tune with Glory, understand our enemy is very good; yes, he is very good in disturbing the body of Christ. But let us get our eyes on the doughnut and not on the hole! Certainly, there are those of us who are cognizant of the lack of genuine love and devotion in the church but will not throw the baby out with the bath water. We are to call attention to the falling away but, at the same time, we must become all things to all men in order to save some. There is an Ephesian church in our midst in this century, but there is a Philadelphian church, as well. James, the brother of our Lord, said it best. In his letter he exposed the body and revealed its shortcomings.

It is here we learn that sweet little Christians told those with physical needs things what they did not need to hear. These shallow Christians overlooked the basic needs of those attending their assemblies. You recall their hollow evangelism when they told those asking for assistance to just be filled and dress warmly. There are dear saints of God who despise the coming holidays, empty Christmases in lonely apartments. They need more than empty phrases. They deserve more. Where is the Church?

It is the message of the book of James that should move us to take inventory and respond to the silent cry of millions who are lonely and would welcome the outstretched arms of compassion. It is not intended to create a guilt trip, by any means, but rather, to awaken us to our God-given responsibility to reach out not only to the lost but to the lonely. There was a period, some eight decades ago, that placed entirely too much emphasis on a social gospel. Today we have become virtually unresponsive to the basic needs of a wounded society. We are interested in seeing the lost find salvation but we have turned a deaf ear to people's heart-felt needs. We are interested in your tithe but don't approach us with your problems and certainly don't share with us your desire for genuine love. It is not that we have become bitter, but we are baffled without question.

And so, let us return to the basics of the Word of God with respect to those who have been neglected by the religious. It does not take much study on our part to discover that we have a Creator who is deeply moved over hurting people within the sacred book. The question remains as to what our response will be to the socio-spiritually sequestered.

First, we must become aware that there is an on-going problem before we can undertake any effective or credible effort to alleviate the pain. It becomes most disturbing that most of our local assemblies are oblivious to the basic needs of our day and few seem to be motivated by the desperation and isolation of the masses.

> "Religion can be used not only to cover up man's hostility and aggression; every so often it veils a special brand of narcissism and becomes an escape from loneliness rather than a tool with which to conquer

it, a cozy nest into which the sufferer retreats when the problems of life become too overwhelming. All the lonesome and frightened men and women who use religion in such a distorted way simply repeat and transpose the very human situation of the neurotic from the earthly plane onto a transcendental level."[3]

Those disturbed by ostracization, whatever the source, find themselves in a quandary leaving them all but helpless, but thankfully, not hopeless. This is precisely why we are investigating the causes and effects of this debilitating, infrequently examined condition.

Serious contemplation of this emotional upheaval may be best understood by those who have had personal experience in this matter. Visiting the Alzheimer's facility, where my bride now resides, I discovered that only a handful of people actually visit their family members who are residents there. Still, even those that do show up for a visit spend inadequate quality time with those afflicted. It would not be kind to report how many "friends" have stopped by to greet my spouse who has been "incarcerated" for over a year.

It is vital to examine all aspects of isolation and sequestering in this transitory time on planet earth. Let us then seek to exhaust all pertinent resources available to us, whether by means of written accounts or through shared personal testimony. Speaking through personal experience, my findings indicate that there may be more revealed in this expose' than in any single book, periodical, or the like.

The general consensus among believers in our locale verify this hypothesis, namely, that churches have almost become hot houses or incubators for the lonely. Personal interviews are most shocking. A young mother in one interview, relates how she visited several Sunday School classes in a local assembly because every class had, what she termed, a clique. While growing to adulthood in North Carolina, I can't recall the word "clique" ever being used, and certainly not to describe the fellowship within the church. Times are changing and so is our socio-spiritual community.

Without a doubt, my God is not excited with His church. We are interested in baptisms, buildings, budgets, and even bountiful growth, but when it comes to being friendly, well, that just isn't a top priority. Some time ago, a well known preacher from our state was traveling with his wife. They passed a small church in their journey that displayed a sign which read, "Harmony Church." "How precious," said the pastor's wife when shortly down the road they were met with a second sign which read, "Harmony Church II." Funny, yes, and yet quite pathetic. This is where we are today and the church needs to experience a revival and quickening from within. Saving souls is commendable, and of the utmost importance. At the same time, our labors in this area must not preclude us from ministering to the needs of the hurting, saved or unsaved. We are ignoring our community's wounded by the score and leaving people behind who are unable to fend for themselves. We gloat over the souls we see saved, at the same time, exerting precious little effort to visit the widows or to care for the homeless. We wonder why folks are lonely and feel as though the world is passing them by. "Only as we can really come in touch with our own humanity can we enter into the humanity of others with real caring and understanding."[4]

> "As we find time to be alone with God, we give Him the opportunity to meet our inner needs. As we are conscious of his doing this, we become more aware of God's desire to meet the needs of those about us. He is constantly preparing us to help meet those needs."[5]

There is still another form of affliction creating loneliness in some lives which needs addressing, as well, in our communities.

It has come to our attention that the people of God, especially in these days of confusion, are under a most subtle form of attack designed by our common enemy. We shall face a legion of obstacles as we draw near to the end times; however, we will address this single issue here, as it can result in further feelings of isolation and abandonment for many individuals. This isolation may find its origin in a relationship that has become an unhealthy symbiotic union. This usually manifests itself when individuals are brought together in a project or task, whereupon they become thoroughly engrossed in such a concerted undertaking that they are not cognizant that they begin to feed on one another. Their weaknesses, which are usually unseen and hidden, begin to receive attention from *one party* to *the other*, or from *both parties* toward *each another*.

After some span of time when those individuals, especially of the opposite sex, are united in a cause of a certain magnitude, it may create an unseen binding together which may not be fully comprehended until some departure or until an emergency arises. It is at this time that an unseen force will bind up one, or both, of these folks. Some have referred to this malady as a corruption of what may be defined as a soul tie. This condition is created by those who have a controlling power similar to that of a reptile which will cast a spell on a bird for it's destruction. This condition may or may not be detected by the individuals prior to the ultimate devastation. A similar situation may arise, in some cases, even when there has not been a prolonged engagement in some concerted task or project. Those who are vulnerable to such a spell may lose their reasoning faculties and their ability to think properly. This may create a complete obsession with the one who is smitten by the enemy resulting in lonesomeness and an empty feeling that causes one to lose their identity and purpose for living.

To mention such an affliction without offering an antidote would be of no help to anyone and exceedingly cruel. When one is plagued by such an attack, they must seek assistance immediately. Often times, the person who falls under the control of the enemy may resort to attempts at suicide in an effort to be freed from their oppression.

Whenever one becomes overwhelmed by the afore mentioned, they must call upon gifted people of God that are knowledgeable of such satanic warfare and who are full of the Holy Spirit. Much effectual intercession over the wounded soul is necessary. They must be anointed with the Holy Spirit as depicted in the administering of oil as seen in James 5:14. It may take repeated meetings with this select group of loving, godly saints to remove this powerful oppression.

The person under bondage must confess their knowledge of the matter which created their condition or misconduct. They are to ask for God's forgiveness. They must ask Him to restore them to their right standing in Jesus Christ. Finally, they need to pray to be filled with the fullness of God's Holy Spirit and for blessed renewal.

If the situation continues, they are to plead that the blood of Christ remove the guilt and defeat the power of Satan completely, taking authority over the evil one as described in passages such as James 4:7 and Ephesians 4:27, 6:11. This most complex and subtle issue will need to be bathed in much prayer, with dedicated people of God, over an extended period. But one can and must be delivered from this dreadful spiritual cancer, creating a swell of joy in the one that is set free.

How exceedingly disturbing to fall into the hands of the enemy. But when we become deceived by a friend, or even worse, a Christian brother, it leaves us wondering, "Where did everyone go?"

It occurred to me in life's experience that a personal friend, who has served Christ as a minister of the Gospel, would be an excellent person to interview. He has been a faithful man of God for almost half a century and highly respected among evangelical believers. The question posed to him was one pertaining to the matter of the "falling away" occurring in our contemporary churches. His response was that there is less camaraderie today and a coldness is growing in the body of Christ. The conclusion, born out of much research in this area, is that we are being summoned to respond. It is a call to arms. This study carries much weight in a day when it is evident that we need to be either hot or cold or we will be suddenly removed. Our concern must be evident in our deep love and genuine devotion to Christ and to our brothers and sisters. The main reason we are losing people from our fellowships is that we lack compassion for one another. We do not know our brethren as we once did when life was much less complex than it is today.

> "There is the bone-breaking loneliness of Adam
> without a partner and the heart-breaking loneliness of
> Abraham and Sarah without a child. There is a young
> man sitting in a pig-yard wondering whether he can
> go home and his brother listening to party-music
> from the road and turning away from the door. And
> there is a young man whose sisters love him so much
> they challenge God; and he lies in a tomb, wrapped
> in so much loneliness that it has been a day since his

spirit left. O look at all the lonely people; their lenting stories are dress rehearsal for Gethsemane, which is the loneliest story of all."[6]

The contributor of this passage, in her magazine article, has given the title of loneliness over to the subject of lent, i.e., "Loneliness is a Four Letter Word."

Loneliness, rejection, sequestering, and abandonment are all alive and well on planet earth. It is being overlooked by most of us who name the Name of Jesus Christ. This is exactly why this subject is being covered. We are sounding an overdue alarm to believers in our generation. The enemy of our souls loves it when individuals fall into the pit of loneliness and he is quick to provide his means of solace.

As one who initially comes to the Savior of their soul out of desperation, so those who have become sequestered by their circumstances feel the pangs of despair. A slap on the back and a verse of scripture is not the real answer, by any means. It has been my experience with some dear Christians that they are quick to provide scripture, but otherwise, they prefer to stay uninvolved. When people do such, they may be sharing the scripture only to placate their own conscience. They then send the desperate soul on his saddened road to what they hope will be a successful recovery. Some Christians are not equipped to help, while others, simply do not care to assist. At such times when Christians provide their scriptures, I provide my special passage, also. I have been known to quote I Chronicles 26:18, "At Parbar westward, four at the causeway, and two at Parbar." Sometimes they understand that what has been offered was meant in jest and they smile in amusement. Others are baffled, so I asked them if they were blessed by what they heard. It becomes obvious, we need to offer more than words.

I realize that many just don't have a clue as how to provide comfort to those struggling with life. Certainly none of us are immune from the situations of life overtaking us and leaving us hurting and vulnerable. Our Lord, Himself, endured many hardships as He walked on this earth. Why would there not be those we know in our churches who are facing desperate times and are in need of a companion? The real reason most of us fail to respond is primarily because we see others experiencing falls and failings but we do not acknowledge our own shortcomings. Therefore, we shirk our responsibility by hiding behind some glorified church activities. We end up becoming the proverbial "ostrich with his head in the sand," in this case, the sand of religiosity. There joinder resounds, "He who pokes his head into the sand makes an excellent target!"

As we delve into the disturbing reality of loneliness, regardless of it's source, we become aware it is a topic that needs serious attention. In visiting libraries to research the subject, I found a dearth of useful printed information. And yet, our society is deluged by the score of individuals suffering from this emotional nightmare. Again, how can we address an issue unless we recognize it for what it is, a crisis that potentially may effect those in every walk of life. Loneliness manifests itself in many facets and unless we are willing to deal with it openly and thoroughly, we will certainly suffer the consequences.

"The illusion that loneliness is 'odd' or 'abnormal' adds to the distress of those who feel it, and may lure into inappropriate 'socializing' people who, if this were not thought 'odd' would be well content to keep their own company."[7] Edgar Johnson, in his article, makes it abundantly clear that loneliness is not at all what the average individual contemplates. The author continues by analyzing the underlying conditions.

"It (loneliness) may be present in the gregarious as well as the solitary, and in the smothering intimacy of village or tenement as well as the anonymity of the city street; that it may be deepened by misguided efforts to overcome it in ourselves or insensitive attempts to revive it in others."[8]

Although little seems to be forthcoming in research with regard to actual books written on the subject, there are some magazine articles available in our archives. In the perusal of libraries, both secular as well as sacred, there is limited information available on the topic. The lack of written material is certainly not a deterrent to those who are aware of this condition which is rampant in our society. Thus, we garner information through all that is available to us in the libraries and by gleaning what we can in personal interviews, from lay people to seasoned clergymen.

One magazine article, though written some thirty years ago, holds valuable commentary on this monstrous emotional dilemma.

> "Loneliness seems to involve the feeling of not only wanting another but also not being wanted by another. Anyone who has sat alone in a bustling cafeteria while other people sit together talking and laughing has probably felt for a moment the interwined twinges of loneliness and wanting to be wanted.
>
> Two basic feelings underline the various forms of loneliness. The first is a lack of the sense of belonging. Not being chosen by others, the lonely person is unsure that he is really wanted by anyone. The second is the feeling that no one understands."[9]

Of the two theories it would seem that the later is more acerbic in nature. When one arrives at a place and time where he or she deems they are misunderstood in a socio-spiritual environment, they are at a place where they need outside intervention. This is where a parachute is essential to rescue the troubled individual and assist them to a safe landing and a secure shelter.

Again, we find that we are ill equipped to meet the on-going maladies of our frustrated communities. Thus, we must first recognize the spiritual conflict and then, of course, be prepared to accompany the afflicted into a safe and secure harbor. Here is where a gifted and qualified counselor has the opportunity to become extremely successful. This counselor, in order to maximize his potential for success, must be a biblical counselor rather than a secular, or even, a mere Christian counselor.

With this before us we should understand the thought process of what may be termed "special people." These are those which have some mental deficiency or disability. These special people can detect almost immediately if a person is genuine or a fake. These individuals can be deeply spiritual and seem to intuitively know if someone is sincere or not. These special believers must seek assistance from God who will direct them to trustworthy counsel. Upon meeting up with those whom the Almighty has supplied to help them, these challenged folks will soon observe that something unique prevails with these dedicated saints. They shall soon learn that these para-helpers, or assistants from God, will deal quite differently with them than others they have encountered. The servant of God will listen, not with their minds alone, but also with their hearts. Furthermore, they will be in tune with their very souls. They will not speak at the person, but with them. They are on the same page; the same wave length. These counselors learn about the individuals they are counseling, but do not judge. They love unconditionally. They do not provide unnecessary advice, or bombard with scriptures. They guide the distressed and the lonely through their turmoil, never abandoning them in their need.

In the book, *Soul Cravings,* Erwin R. McManus speaks on the subject, "One is the Loneliest Number" and this topic became vital in my quest for additional support.

> "Have you ever come face to face with the vacuum of love that exists within your soul? Have you ever had an unexplained sense of loneliness even while you're standing in the middle of a crowd? At the same time you can be all by yourself and have a wonderful sense of connectedness with the world. You can enjoy being alone, but you are the one person who simply could not be loved or was somehow born unworthy of love? Sometimes we'll go to unimaginable extremes to earn love, to feel love, to be loved. Without love, every night is a three-dog night."[10]

It has been said that misery loves company, and at times we must agree. It is somewhat comforting that there are those who have become acquainted with similar sorrows; we know we are not alone. However, we should not be satisfied by the knowledge that we share the depths of despair with others. Our goal should be to overcome and to assist others into the place of completeness and wholeness in Christ.

There is a certain void within all of us which may be filled with either goodness or evil. This should awaken us to seek after that which is right and proper for all concerned. This is precisely why we are being confronted with the topic of the socio-sequestered soul. We are examining how individuals fall prey to loneliness and its debilitating effects as well as discussing solutions to this dilemma in which many find themselves. This common, but seldom studied emotion, is most sinister in nature. It is, therefore, incumbent upon all of us to provide more attention to the subject at hand lest we fail in correcting this socio-spiritual crisis.

We must examine Paul's most comprehensive writing, the book of Romans. If we claim Romans 8:28 then we must agree that God will use our sequestering to His, and ultimately our, advantage. I recall an exceptional spiritual leader counseling with a lady who had inadvertently run over a little girl who subsequently died from her injuries. This distraught believer in Christ was comfortless in what had happened. In the good counsel of this godly man he reminded her of Paul's teaching. She was questioned as to her solid understanding and acceptance of "all things work together for good." She could not understand the reason but, nevertheless, she understood that she needed to accept what happened "in all things." It was upon allowing this counsel to penetrate the depths of her innermost soul that she surrendered and came to accept what, at first, she could not accept.

In our respective lives, for the most part, when all seems to be running rather smoothly we fail to rely on God. We somehow imagine ourselves as little, self-sufficient gods with little or no need for God. We sort of run on automatic, that is until we run amok. It is then we will usually begin to wonder what is happening in our lives. We start to realize that we have lost control. Our God seems to be a foreign God and we feel as though we are wandering in a foreign, uncharted land.

When the lonesomeness settles in around and about us, it is in such times that we really want to hear the sweet voice of God. It is at this juncture that we observe a decided demarcation of individuals. One group seems to lean toward working their way out of the maze. This group tends to believe that God does not speak to man as He once did. Then there is still another faction which will rely on the Lord to assist them to a place of refuge. This group of individuals tend to believe that God does speak today in much the same manner as He did in the past.

For those who read the comics, and many still do, there was a cartoon recently which depicts this understanding of our Lord. The cartoonist is Johnny Hart who writes the comic strip, B.C. Typically during Christmas, Easter, and other sacred holidays, Hart will share a spiritual message via his comic strip. On March 25, 2007, the premise in the comic was that of God speaking "in the now." Two girls, in the first frame of his comic, go to the mountain where the first girl claims she talks to God. The second girl is skeptical. God indeed speaks, and the skeptic wonders if the voice they heard was truly God. The last frame tells the story that is essential as God declares, "I get that a lot lately!"

God is trying to get through to us in various ways. Sometimes He answers not a word. It is all too quiet as we are wanting to hear from Him alone. During these times when we feel abandoned, when we believe we are forgotten, He can finally get through to us. In dealing with the counselees who fit this description, we who counsel are at a decided advantage. Those who counsel are at their best when they, too, have gone through the silent treatment.

> "Meanwhile, where is God? This is one of the most disquieting symptoms. When you are happy, so happy that you have no sense of needing Him, so happy that you are tempted to feel His claims upon you as an interruption, if you remember yourself and turn to Him with gratitude and praise, you will be - or so it feels- welcomed with open arms. But go to Him when your need is desperate, when all other help is in vain, and what do you find? A door slammed in your face, and a sound of bolting and double bolting on the inside. After that silence."[11]

It does not take the expertise of a rocket scientist to discover that the God who is at work in the writings of C.S. Lewis is also at work in the writing of this updated chronicle. The crux of the matter is in an individual allowing God to reveal to him the reason for his isolation. And yet, doubtless, there are multitudes of dear people who will not discover the reason for their turmoil until they reach the shores of eternity. At that point there will be no need for any questions as we behold Him face to face. He shall wipe away every tear from our once blinded eyes. Those questions we deemed to be paramount in this life will be overshadowed on that glorious day when we bow before Jehovah God.

CHAPTER THREE

Desperate in the Scenario

In God's divine providence I discovered a medical physician who was willing to assist in the care of my spouse who had become afflicted with Alzheimer's. The gifted doctor was one who had expertise in the aging process. Being directed by his Lord, he had discovered valuable treatment strategies for those suffering with dementia. Unfortunately, my wife's condition had deteriorated to such a point that the good doctor was unable to achieve any measurable results in her particular case. However, he did help me place my wife in a long term care facility in March 2006. He has been an enormous blessing to me. A close relationship developed between us due to the commonality of experiences shared, born of life's demands and struggles.

What the doctor and I didn't realize was that we were unwittingly bartering. God was using him to help me make my way through the difficult events unfolding in my life, while, at the same time, God was allowing me to provide counsel to this dear physician and his wife. However, by April of that year it became evident that I would no longer be able to engage in any serious counseling. The trauma surrounding my wife's illness had caused tremendous emotional upheaval in my life. When my doctor friend learned what had brought about my decision to end our counseling sessions, he whisked me away to a haven in Charleston. He realized that neither he, as a physician, nor myself, as a counselor, had the wherewithal to deal with the turmoil that had now become an insurmountable roadblock in my life.

Arriving in the environs of Charleston, we met with a devoted godly couple who ministered to me in my conflicted emotional state which seemed plagued by the demonic. Without any conversation, the scriptures were opened to a story in Matthew's account. It related how that the Apostle Peter was at sea and ran into a storm that was evidently not of his, nor of his Master's making. How did God travel to South Carolina and bring an answer to my plight without anyone's foreknowledge? The answer may well be revealed in a prayer that was prayed shortly before this event. The prayer I prayed was this:

"Dear God, I have thoroughly enjoyed the Book you wrote. When I am in need of a primer to approach you in conversation, there is that one hundred and fifty chapter chronicle. And when there is need for admonishment, again, I turn to that collection of thirty one Proverbs. Then, when I wish to truly understand the Messiah, I usually read His sermon, which is not as lengthy as most I have heard and is certainly never boring. Much of Your great Book I have memorized and I recite it when an occasion arises. You have a way of speaking to me through its pages, which is magnificent.

But do You know what? I'm very lonely and really need a personal visit. This is a strange request, but perhaps, there have been stranger ones. You see, I really need a real live person right now that I can hug and sit down and talk with. You have done this before, as I have read in Your delightful written Word. So why not surprise me and do a repeat performance in *our* time?

And yet, as I give this more thought, I understand that if You were to answer such a request and were to come, and then leave, I would be more upset and feel more lonely than ever before. Thus, I am to be content as I lean upon the Holy Spirit to bring me what is needful until I get to meet You face to face. But somehow, just writing this has assisted me in more fully comprehending You, as well as, myself. Possibly, we may pass this on to others who have similar feelings, also, which for some reason they have been unable to express."

I felt as though God was answering that very prayer as the scriptures were opened before me and as these dear saints of God shared His love. The minister's wife went on to speak about a painting that the couple had hanging in their home which touched the very heart of my plight. She related that it was a painting depicting the disciples in the boat while Peter and the Christ were in the turbulent waters. "You, Peter, are 'second Peter' and you are at sea, as well. As with the Apostle Peter, so with you; your emotions are spent. You are bewildered and beset due to all that has transpired in this separation from your wife." It was further related to me that my distress was understandable human sorrow but that my eyes were on my problem and not on the Person. Once we allow ourselves to discover the real reasons for our loneliness, we begin to see gloom dispelled and transformed into gladness by His healing hand.

There was even more information to be unveiled by this God-provided couple. One valuable lesson came as they shared a passage from the Gospel of John. The minister and his wife reported, in concert, that a thief and robber had come to kill, rob and destroy the servant of God that now sat before them. As we delved into the biblical account contained in John chapter ten, we immediately ascertained that this was, undeniably, what was happening to me. Every tactic was being implemented by the enemy with crippling results. We all marveled at such a divine revelation. God, it seemed, was at work answering my impassioned plea after all.

The plot thickens. Get prepared for a new thing that God is doing in our midst and in our day. As God spoke to Samuel, and Eli was puzzled, so it is in our day. God is speaking but we are not listening (Hebrews 5:11).

As the doctor and I left South Carolina to return home, God was speaking to my heart, to my mind, and to my very soul. He was about to unveil an even greater manifestation of His glory that same day. Neither of us knew what the Lord had in store for us that very evening. As we arrived at home in Raleigh, my friend suggested that we attend a service at a local church. Complete strangers to this particular church, my friend, a friend of his, and I sat down in this small white clapboard facility that housed an entire black congregation. The guest minister was late, so while we waited, the ushers took up two offerings. My rejoinder to God and to man at this juncture was one of skepticism.

What did God have in mind in all of this? The meeting, however, was not governed by time but by eternity. When the minister finally arrived, he went to the sacred desk and asked the congregation to turn in their Bibles to the same two accounts that had been brought to our attention the day before in Charleston! The minister repeated precisely what had been revealed to us only one day before in South Carolina. My friend turned to me and asked me if I now believed that God had shown up on my doorstep and whether or not I now believed it was possible for God to manifest Himself in our day. The day of miracles had not ceased.

Please pass the tissues! Tears flowed like a river of joy. God had manifested Himself in a way that we had not previously witnessed. God will show up in our lonely lives if we will stop, look, and listen. It seems that He will wait until the very last second to arrive; He makes us wait but He is never late. These two accounts had several witnesses. Only two witnesses are required, but several witnesses are able to attest to these unbelievable events. If this was only one man's testimony there might be reason to doubt but certainly not with many witnesses.

Searching my soul and the computer in my study of isolation, desperation, and loneliness led to emptiness, for the most part. The world's solution to the subject springs from the flesh and not the spirit. It is a dead end street leaving little or no margin for a U-turn toward right choices. Some suggest that loneliness may lead to Alzheimer's but in my case it was Alzheimer's that was leading me to feel the pangs of loneliness. One on-line article, however, offered a welcomed perspective to the topic of loneliness.

> "Perhaps the most common malady of the soul in our sophisticated age today is loneliness. And because Jesus became man, He shares in the full range of our feelings. Although He traveled with the disciples for several years, they seldom communicated on the same wave length. When He hung on the cross, He uttered these horrible words, 'My God, My God, Why have

You forsaken Me?' (Matthew 27:46). Jesus can help you during your bouts with loneliness. The first man, Adam, was alone in the Garden of Eden; but there was no indication that he was ever lonely. Quite the opposite seemed evident. He enjoyed the exquisite communion with the Father, who provided him with a helpmate, Eve, because . . . 'it is not good for the man to be alone . . .' (Genesis 2:18). Loneliness of spirit began when Adam and Eve sinned in the Garden of Eden. He (man) is lonely to some extent because he has not found another person with whom he can share his burdens."[1]

Allow me to share with you where my heart is in the topic that is before us. I usually place my tropical fish in the tank by pairs. They seem to fare better this way than if left alone. There are many of God's creatures that, when losing their mates, will not seek to find another mate for the remainder of their lives. (These are not found in Hollywood, however.)

When alone in a house, which was once our home, a sadness will close in from many dimensions. The sound of a locomotive in the distant fog. Even romantic music once loved is turned off because of a pain that cannot be alleviated or quelled. Most of all, when lifting a voice of praise in the sanctuary of God, a hymnal is no longer shared with a mate. It is here, when tears accumulate, that a strong awakening for God to intervene leads to a genuine worship of the One who genuinely empathizes with the souls of man. All gloom is dispelled when Jesus comes to us and we worship Him alone. Thus, any loneliness from any source is subdued by His presence. Again, whenever one is called to a life of solitude, God will often times employ such to draw His own into deeper fellowship and a more passionate worship.

One ingredient sorely missing from the present day body of believers is thoughtful communication. Within the church there is little patience for those suffering from isolation, regardless of the origin. People do need people. "Even the church bears the mark of this misguided value structure with ever-increasing emphasis

:ational structure for ministry rather than on organic,
1s connections of people ministering to one another."[2]
As we engage in this study we discover that others are experiencing
what we have experienced. There is a definite malady in the Christian
church which, up until now, has either not been noticed or not
addressed. Believers are being isolated in their own places of worship.
We have lost our way and need to return to the basic principles
of New Testament camaraderie or we will fail in our obedience to
Christ's commands. "Friendships drift into functional partnerships
instead of the actual sharing of life. Into this vacuum of disassociated
souls, the New Rebellion raises a vision once again for authentic
community."[3]

In order to more fully appreciate the two sentences just quoted,
you must be in the current fray. By becoming involved, you may
discover that in this new century the Christian community has left
untold numbers of believers destitute. Scriptures exhorting us to
care for the widow are being disregarded. Holidays become horror
days. Isolation is rampant and will continue to grow until someone
stands up and calls the body of Christ to attention. Many churches
are involved in expansion and fund raising for larger buildings while,
unbeknownst to others, strife and power struggles are raging. Does
not the news of thousands of clergy leaving their ministries send a
message that things are amiss in the church?

Were the body of Christ being led solely by the Holy Spirit, we
would discover the disappearance of welfare, as we know it. There is no
group of people so sequestered as those relying on public assistance.
We must ask ourselves, "Are those that call themselves 'Christians'
in our churches *true* believers?" Not all that claim to be "Christians"
are necessarily believers, while all true believers may certainly be
referred to as Christians. Those who are God's children by grace must
arise and reach the destitute and all those who feel forsaken by this
cold world in which we live. We must not expect non-believers to do
the work of Christ; it is incumbent upon the true believers to answer
the call. He that has ears, let him hear and respond to the high call
of God. God has commissioned us to free slaves sequestered by the
neglect of the very people who should be serving their soon coming
Deliverer.

In a well known theological seminary, seminary students were assigned the passage of scripture commonly referred to as the parable of the Good Samaritan. Each one, studying and preparing to go out and minister to this needy world, was asked to write and preach a sermon on this memorable story found in Luke's gospel.

Every seminarian worked feverishly, I'm sure, to perfect their final drafts. The day arrived when each seminarian was prepared to deliver his message, lauding the admirable qualities of love and neighborly concern that the Good Samaritan in the parable conveys. As the students hurried to the chapel to give their respective messages, someone, unbeknownst to the students, had a brilliant revelation. This individual stationed a man near the path to the chapel who appeared to be in dire need of medical attention. These brilliant theological candidates saw the need before them, but no one stopped to assist. Without exception, the students passed by, relating that they were unable to help at that particular moment. The students' empty explanations were understood to mean that they were in a big hurry to preach a sermon and didn't have time to help a desperately needy individual.

This illustration depicts what we find all too often in today's churches. We are witnessing a day of emptiness, busyness, and utter isolationism. We are so engrossed in our own affairs that we are oblivious to the social and spiritual needs of those secluded and ultimately withdrawn in bewilderment.

> "Spiritual abuse is the mistreatment of a person who is in need of help, support or greater spiritual empowerment, with the result of weakening, undermining or decreasing that person's spiritual empowerment."[4]

This afore quoted statement was published in the latter part of this century and was a precursor to current day matters which we are addressing in this study. Beloved, we have become remiss in our mission of providing an antidote for the poison in our society. We have abandoned man beside the highway of life and gone away in our preoccupation with secondary things. However, all is not lost, for where there is spiritual life and conscience, we can certainly come to the place where God can use us. This will be accomplished as we comprehend where we are and understand where we need to be. Jesus reminds us that whenever we dry a widow's tears or visit a lonely soul, we have ultimately done it unto Him. What an awakening this creates in our souls when we understand that, in the final analysis, we have become obedient to God's call on our lives.

However, in order to fully understand our situation, we need to revisit the account of the Good Samaritan. In the scenario, as delivered by Christ, there were three observers of the wounded traveler. Two of the three passersby represented the religious clientele; the third man was a representative of genuine spirituality. Religion is deadly and exhibited its character in the denial of the One who came to save those stripped by the enemy of their souls. Thus, it shall forever behoove those of us, who are true believers, to avoid religiosity by all means and cleave to the Redeemer. We need to glorify Christ by "being there" for those who have been left to die in their misery.

In her compassionate writings, Elizabeth Kübler-Ross, M.D., may help us better understand the plight of those who feel the wrenching effects of isolation. Perhaps her medical expertise can add a depth of understanding to what we are viewing from a purely theological side.

> "When the staff (dealing with one dying) contributed to her isolation, we tended to be angry at them and made it a routine to keep the door open, only to find it closed again on our next visit. As we became more familiar with her peculiarities, they appeared less strange to us and began to make more sense, adding to our difficulties in appreciating the nurses' needs to avoid her. Towards the end it became a personal matter, a feeling of sharing a foreign language with someone who was unable to communicate with others."[5]

Isolation from others, in life or death, need not become the solution for any person dealing with the bitter pain of loneliness. Has it ever occurred to us that the Lord, Himself, became lonesome? Why were we created? Was it not to enjoy fellowship with others and with our God? Jesus questioned His disciples as to their lack of desire to be with Him in His deepest period of isolation in Gethsemane. Jesus reported that he was lowly. He may not just have been revealing His meekness, but expressing an innermost yearning for communion with the humanity He created. We, being made in His image, have an innate need for fellowship, breathed into us by Christ.

There is a story of a poor man lost for years on a deserted island. Although he was all alone, he erected three buildings in the days that he spent in seclusion. One day, rescuers arrived. The rescuers, seeing this lone inhabitant, questioned the man on the three buildings he had constructed. "Well, of course, this building where we now stand is where I sleep", he replied. "The building next to it is where I worship." The rescuers seemed satisfied with these answers and then asked about the third building. His sad reply, "Oh, that is where I *used* to worship."

Some dear souls seem to be a island unto themselves. However, God has so fashioned us that we have a certain spot within us which cannot be filled by any other means than by God alone. Place a large seashell up to your ear and you can hear the roar of the ocean as if it is longing for its original home. We need God. We need to have fellowship with God and with one another. Our common enemy is doing all that is in his power to thwart this very longing in our souls. Satan's plan is to divide and conquer. It was his original plan in the Garden of Eden; it is still his plan today. Lucifer's strategy is to discourage, divide, defeat, and destroy and in doing so, he will send souls into solitary confinement according to his devious devices to undo them.

With this before us, we turn to a statement extricated from another's findings in *Emotional Intelligence*.

"A key social ability is empathy, understanding other's feelings and taking their perspective, and respecting differences in how people feel about things. Relationships are a major focus, including learning to be a good listener and question-asker, distinguishing between what someone says or does and your own reactions and judgments, being assertive rather than angry or passive; and learning the arts of cooperation, conflict resolution, and negotiating compromises."[6]

A few Christmas seasons ago, we received a personal note included inside a traditional Christmas card. The reason for citing this correspondence, is to emphasize how we, as humans, need one another and need to be open in our response to how others relate to us. In our journey to reach out to hurting people, we need to respect their feelings and deep-seated needs.

This precious saint of God from New Jersey, wrote in her Christmas note a detailed description of her troubles. She opened the letter by saying that she had gone to the doctor and he had determined she had developed uterine cancer. She went on to relate that her mother's cat had just passed away with kidney failure and they were all saddened. She continues by sharing the story of her operation and on-going radiation treatments for her cancer.

This dear lady had no intention of being humorous, but her story was so incredible and the way she told it, so matter-of-fact, you weren't sure if you should laugh or cry! But it doesn't stop there! She goes on to tell of her spouse being held-up at knife point, bound with duct tape and blindfolded. Three days later her husband lost his job after twenty-seven years of employment. Then, she goes on to relate how she had to return to work because of her husband's lost income and reports that her family was left without medical coverage. She ends her letter by writing of her mother's blackouts on Halloween and how she would love to go to church in a sleigh! (Knowing her is delightful!)

For years I have kept this note which has helped me to laugh when I've needed encouragement and needed to lighten-up. One once remarked, "O how foolish we mortals be." We are but, at the same time, even God has a keen sense of humor. He displays it even though we do not always recognize this side of His nature in our daily dealings with Him.

In order to summarize and pull together what we are being asked to consider, we are to love and enjoy our Creator. At the same time, we must not allow ourselves to become isolated or withdrawn. We are in a learning process which is equipping us for an eternity which is awesome.

> "God had designed us for relationship not only with himself but also with others of our kind. After God created the world, He stepped back to look at His work and pronounced it 'very good.' However, before His creation was complete, He said one thing - and only one - was not good. 'It is not good for the man to be alone. I will make a helper suitable for him.' (Genesis 2:18). God planned for Adam, and all mankind, to need human companionship. In other words, God made people to need and desire others besides himself."[7]

In all of our desperation, we must come to the conclusion that God, in His unfathomable dealings with us, will allow us to walk through periods of utter grief and unsettling loneliness. It is not that He has forgotten us but is drawing us unto Himself through silence, quietness, temporary withdrawal or whatever means He, in His infinite wisdom, deems necessary. This may seem strange, and possibly, unacceptable; however, the only means of proving the matter is in our own personal commitment to our God and in our devotion to the lonely and forsaken who we meet daily as we sojourn here.

Man may, at times, become paralyzed by unwanted and uncertain kinds of desperation. At every juncture he is beset by what may be insurmountable, comparable to a Red Sea experience. Our "Red Sea" may not be as cooperative as former servants of the Almighty found it to be! Where is God in all of this? We want out! If God seems to be a foreigner, we need to ask ourselves, "Who took the journey?" Often we feel as though God has abandoned us, when we are guilty of abandoning Him. It is God who desires our close fellowship; He wants to embrace us, but it becomes difficult to hug a porcupine; don't you agree?

> "So let us begin our solution to the problem of loneliness with the cultivation of creative solitude. Risk

being alone with yourself as a venture in discovery. Getting in touch with ourselves gets us in touch not only with our own humanity but with all humanity. Our pains are also other's pains; our pleasures are also their pleasures. Creative solitude is actually a base for community because it is the basis for our identity with humanity. We take our creative solitude with us into the world. It stays with us in the midst of people. Creative solitude establishes relationships with others. In *Reaching Out,* Henri Nouwen puts it well: 'The movement from loneliness to solitude... creates the inner space where a compassionate solidarity with our fellow human beings becomes possible.'"[8]

As we conclude this chapter, we are discovering that a multitude of various authors are providing credence to this treatise. We are not daydreamers or on a tangent. Paul, in I Corinthians 9:26 addresses his listeners, perhaps out of frustration, saying that he did not engage in shadow boxing like some aimless fanatic. There is eternal purpose to this study of loneliness. We are confronting an issue that has long been neglected by society, our spiritual leaders, and the church at large. The question remains: "What are we going to do with this information that we are now being asked to confront?"

CHAPTER FOUR

Doldrums Due to Emotional Stress

In the early morning, while musing upon the written Word, some birds flew into my field of vision. As a "would-be" ornithologist, I recalled that the birds recorded in Psalm 102:6 and 7 all present a basic theme. The pelican, owl and the sparrow are all alone and proclaim a melancholy melody. I suppose that this could be considered an oxymoron, and I tend to agree. The noted Bible scholar, Matthew Henry, states that, "In affliction, we should sit alone, to consider our ways (Lamentations 3:28) but not sit alone to indulge in inordinate grief."[1]

We, like the Psalmist, become as that little bird perched on the peak of some house-top, or upon the pinnacle of a temple. We are all alone with our thoughts, pondering our next catch or brooding over an empty nest. However, we have been cautioned to avoid self-inflicted wounds of sorrow and grief when we find ourselves alone. All this is easy to say, but then, reality sets in and, once again, we are alone with our thoughts. Upon facing the advancing doldrums, when one's spirit begins to sink, there must be a safe harbor to sail into. A place where we may be alone but surrounded, encircled by a competent and consoling cloud of experienced witnesses.

In reflecting over all that has been discussed in previous chapters, we can see how loneliness leaves us in an unyielding quagmire. When up to our necks in alligators, should we seek to drain the swamp? If one has experienced fully the throes of abandonment, they will surely appreciate the course on which we are about to embark, although it may be quite a roller coaster ride.

We may be lonely due to lack of human fellowship or we may find ourselves left alone with our innermost thoughts and trepidations. In either case, whether we comprehend it or not, we need to draw from a source that is greater than ourselves. As one observant author wrote, "Success is never final, failure is never fatal; it is courage to continue that counts."[2] Elijah thought he faced his enemy solo, however, he found that even though he *thought* he was alone the facts proved otherwise. (Romans 11:3). God and you become a majority in any and every situation. This truth brings much comfort, especially to those who feel alone.

Therefore, all those who are studying in the field of isolation and loneliness are called upon to enter the school of Christ where there are no graduates. The school colors are black and blue, yet the flag must be held high and erect in the battle that we will ultimately win. The battle comes into focus through the testimony of C.S. Lewis when he made this observation,

> "The full acting out of the self's surrender to God demands pain: this action, to be perfect, must be done from the pure will to obey, in the absence, or in the teeth, of inclination. How impossible it is to enact the surrender of self by doing what we like, I know very well from my own experience at the moment."[3]

We need, also, to recall that our Lord Jesus Christ faced being alone many times throughout His earthly ministry. At times it was by choice, which was prescribed and beneficial. Still again, there were periods in His experience with humanity that He was alone due to blatant abandonment. As Christ's followers, we should chart his steps and discover when we need to be alone and how to act when we are abandoned.

As we have noted previously, there is a scarcity of written materials dealing with the plight of the lonely individual. There seems to be a surplus of resources dealing with depression and anxiety, while the plight of the lonely seems to have been omitted. This is distressing because loneliness is a major factor in depression and the root cause of much anxiety.

Multitudes of sequestered people suffer from a sheer lack of proper communication. They are lost in indifference and due to their inability to communicate their inner feelings they end up in utter isolation. Most counselees visit with the counseling community primarily to converse with those who will listen. A gifted biblical counselor will pick up on this and provide not only good counsel but means to a proper solution. Let's not complicate the issue by dismissing loneliness or by calling it by some unpronounceable name; a new disorder concocted by over zealous psychologists and psychiatrists. Let us recognize the need for individuals to be heard and understood, and may this message throw new light on a subject lost in darkness. It seems there is a growing need in our society to stop and appreciate the fragrances that surround us at times. We are so engaged in being engaged that we fail to smell the roses.

> "When we twenty-first century Americans are told to wait for the Lord, it's something of a challenge for us. We live in a culture where everything comes fast. We don't want to wait. We want what we want when we want it. We feel we deserve it, whether we can afford it or not. When it comes to interest rates and monthly payments, we're like Scarlett O'Hara. 'I'll think about it tomorrow.'"[4]

Let us take time to rediscover community: where people do need people. What's the rush? The Psalmist speaks of still waters. Jesus treats His believers as sheep and He left the flock to attend to a little one who had gone astray. We have gone after the masses and left the wounded to fend for themselves. If you like large gatherings, you will fall in love with the modern day mega churches. Perhaps it is time to take journalistic license and swim against the stream of religious majority, regardless of what others may think.

One major contribution to the havoc of socio-spiritual sequestering in our churches is massive congregations. Individualism is swallowed up in the mega church. Did someone, somewhere, sometime ago say, "Fear not, little flock?" Mangers and little towns have grown into huge stables and great cities where individuals are groping for a warm and personal touch. Stop and consider where we are in today's society and suddenly it becomes apparent that we are setting ourselves up for isolation, *personified*. We are not getting better by getting bigger. We are contributing to a growing faction of people who are getting lost in the shuffle. A certain sign of ultimate doom is evident as we become like ships, passing each other in the dark of night in the midst of a growing fog. Does one dare revisit Babel and learn that God is desirous of our spreading out horizontally, not in building vertically in massive multi-million dollar facilities? Believers could reduce indigentcy in our time, drastically, if we spent God's money or the tithe properly. When Christ returns, He will not be rapturing our massive buildings. A voice crying in the wilderness of this age pleads for a return to community and fellowship. This is just one small step towards healing the emotionally distressed of our time. It stands to reason that we can best minister to others and avoid sequestering if we deal with individuals as opposed to the masses. Christ met with Nicodemus one on one. He spoke individually to the woman at the well. Zaccheus learned that he, individually, mattered to the Savior. When Jesus called His disciples, He drew them one by one.

With this in mind, let us look over the shoulder of a man who cautions against man's obsession to reach many while trampling those deemed insignificant. " While they may appreciate the intensity and gustiness of John the Baptist, they recognize that a solitary voice in the desert has less effect than a united voice in the marketplace."[5] In other words, the world continues to promote the theory that largeness outweighs the lone servitude of one individual no matter how dedicated to God and how determined the individual may be. As we continue to grow our church memberships, we often shoot our wounded; neglecting our widows and avoiding our bereft. As repetition aids learning, let me say it again; we are not to become bitter but we should be exceedingly baffled that we allow this travesty to continue in our day.

As we pursue further the slippage of the sequestered into doldrums, it is noteworthy to mention that there may be situations when individuals will self-destruct. When one decides to separate from friends and family for no plausible reason, there is reason to believe that serious trouble lies right around the bend. If this person does not get good godly counsel, he may well slip into depression or another form of compromised mental health.

Stop momentarily and take inventory. Have we not been awakened to a decidedly new concept of what plagues humanity, especially in our church communities? We have all heard the question, "If a tree fall in the forest and no one is there to hear it fall, does it really make a noise?" Is the message of the plight of sequestered souls falling on listening ears? Have we distanced ourselves so far from the hurting that they are like the tree in the uninhabited forest, with no ear to hear their cry for help? Our hearts must respond suddenly to Christ's question: "When the Son of Man returns, will He find faith on the earth?" (Luke 18:8).

Keep in mind that everything is now in place for Christ's sudden return. You should understand that what we are facing may be the apostasy. Let us be true to our calling and sincere in our service to Christ. We have a world filled with massive religious structures and air waves filled with the gospel messages but while the infrastructure may be firmly in place, one question remains. "Have we lost the Spirit of Christ?" This author firmly believes that we have, for the most part, failed to provide the basic love of God for others. We have missed the mark, beloved, and this is a call from the wilderness to return to our first love for God and our fellow man. This message is for those who desire to walk in the light, as He is in the light, determined to live so that the lonely will be drawn to Him as summer bugs to an electric light! The Spirit of God is speaking and if we fail to heed this message, we shall become of all people most miserable. But as I look around, there are some who have caught a glimpse of what God seeks to impart as this age draws to a close.

> "Jesus did not die on the cross to fill church auditoriums, to enable magnificent church campuses to be filled, or to motivate people to implement innovative programs. He died because He loves you and me, He wants an everlasting relationship with us, and He expects that connection to be as all-consuming that we become wholly transformed - Jesus clones, if you will indulge that expression."[6]

Somehow, someway, it must dawn upon our innermost spirit that we are now embarking upon a new church age. This must be an age that is Christ centered, fully dedicated to reaching out to all those left behind in churchianity; sequestered in the trivial paraphernalia of the church that has lost the heart of the original message of our Master.

Growing up in the state of North Carolina and attending a Methodist Church as a young person has provided me insight into the unengaged church culture in which we find ourselves today. The primary ministry of that particular church was meeting the political and social needs of the community. The salvation message was conspicuously absent, and many golden opportunities to reach the lost for Christ were missed. However, it seems that in trying to compensate for those missed opportunities, the pendulum has swung all the way in the other direction. Now churches are focused on seeing souls saved but don't really want to deal with the many issues that are raised by having new converts in the church. And people who have been in the church for years; they should be able to handle their own problems. Loneliness? The message that many are getting from their church is, "Get over it." Where is the compassion in that attitude? We are called upon to be a friend to the friendless. We must come out of our theological shells and embrace all who are suffering with the compassion of Christ. We must see souls saved, but we, also, must see souls set free from epidemic of loneliness sweeping our society.

> "We all face times of feeling abandoned and lonely. Counselors tell us that the number one problem plaguing people today isn't fear, insecurity, or rejection. It's loneliness. Isolation. Longing for

companionship. I was talking with a woman recently who said, "I've been lonely since I was a little girl. Ever since I can remember, I've felt isolated and alone."[7]

As we read other accounts, we discover that there is a certain under current swelling in our society which supports the theme of the socio-spiritually sequestered in this generation. If you had knowledge that a bridge had been destroyed and failed to warn on-coming traffic, that would be considered gross negligence, if not a criminal offense. That is where we stand today as a church. Someone needs to sound the alarm. Paul exhorts the Corinthian believers, "For if the trumpet gives an uncertain sound, who shall prepare himself to the battle?" (I Corinthians 14:8) In all too many places of worship we are getting uncertain sounds. There was an individual who visited the Church of Christ. When leaving the facility, he asked when they were anticipating Christ's visit, as he had not experienced the presence of the God of all Creation during his time in the building.

Beloved, if you are a redeemed believer, then you and I are a part of the Body of Christ. We are the church. No, the church is not a building, the building is only a meeting place. Therefore, we who are members of His body must be God's best representation on planet earth. It behooves us to befriend the friendless. Our Lord Jesus Christ identifies friendship in John 15 as the ultimate call, both in and out of the structural environment. We are not slaves to man, but we are to be friends. The dictionary defines the word, "friend," in this way: "a person on the same side in a struggle."[8] This author's definition is: "someone who knows all about you and loves you anyway." Sadly, this concept is no longer paramount in the great majority of churches. The larger the churches get, the more difficult it becomes to discover a genuine friend within their walls. If this is not the case in your particular church, you are most fortunate. However, if you were to visit other churches, you would soon discover unapproachable and unwelcoming atmospheres; they are legion.

While reading a book by Ron Mehl, I discovered that another brother has been enlightened. He lists several means of turning our bad experiences of loneliness into something good.

"First, realize that our loneliest moments may be arranged by God. Second, decide in advance how you will face those inevitable periods of loneliness and isolation. Third, let your loneliness sensitize you to the heartache of others. A mom sitting by a window waiting for her runaway to come home. A foreign student on a strange American campus. A newly-widowed woman in a Bible class full of couples. A divorced dad unlocking the door of his dark and empty apartment. Fourth, use those times as a prompt to reach out beyond yourself."[9]

Do you get the chill-bumps when the band is playing a patriotic Sousa march and the American flag passes into view? Such is precisely how this article should make us feel. We are now deeply engaged in the study of the doldrums of sequestering and are seeing before us the genuine meaning of what God wants us to experience. That is, namely, to love our neighbor as we love ourselves. The antidote for loneliness, depression, and the sequestering of souls is to fall in love with the lover of our souls and to express this same love by pulling up, emotionally and spiritually, other troubled souls from the quagmire of abandonment and despair.

The brother of our Lord takes us to task in the book of James, telling us, in essence, how we may become "super Christians." He goes on to relate, (I am paraphrasing), how we can just tell the cold and hungry to "stay positive, dress warmly and get a bite to eat. And, by the way, don't sit in my pew." We constantly pass by folks and refuse to reach out with meaningful assistance. This oblivion is the justification for our discussion. The desperate individual has all but been forgotten in our self-absorption.

We must not lose sight of the fact that those of us who are true believers in Christ are His church. Inasmuch as we are a part of this precious body, we are to get off of our sofas, get up from our pews, and venture forth to comfort the comfortless in this thoughtless society. Remember, as we minister to the hurting around us, we are not serving them alone; we are also serving Christ. Consider these remarks in a sermon by Louis Paul Lehman:

"I admire also her (Mary's) desire, she wanted to be near Jesus and to spare Him from indecency. She could not bear to think that they had been parted or that His body should fall into the hands that would misuse it. I cannot understand how you can profess to believe in and love Jesus and yet be content to be apart from Him. She wanted to save Him from any possible abuse. Every gossiping Christian tongue could be stopped on this one truth: What hurts the child of God hurts Jesus."[10]

While visiting in Southern California in the late 50's, it was my pleasure to happen upon another theologian, Dr. Vernon McGee. His salient remarks were shocking to this young preacher. He exhorted his congregation to be careful not to mention anything they did not want repeated by people in his congregation. "Furthermore," he said, "we have cavemen here who shall drag you into their caves and club you to death!" Still another man of God is witness to the ill treatment of individuals by "Christians" a half-century ago.

It is extremely vital for us to be a friend to those who are by themselves and need our attention. We must be vigilant in our determination not to cause those dear souls to be exposed to gossip or ridicule. This is one of the most insidious forces inflicting agony upon the sequestered of our society. These kinds of travesties lead to a listlessness in the lives of those with whom we wish to have some influence.

Those of us, who are deeply concerned about extricating suffering souls from their sequestering, must come to understand the underlying causes for such a dilemma if we ever hope to meet with success. No one likes to deal with puss, but before a wound can heal properly, the infection must be addressed. This is precisely the reason for delving into the real reason why we are killing our wounded. Why thousands, literally thousands of clergy have resigned or gone on to other professions. Why people are leaving churches and changing their memberships. Not all of our churches are experiencing genuine revival. People may have not been *transformed* but may have merely *transferred* from one assembly to another. And while we are gloating

rgeoning church attendance, the widow goes unvisited. The
ul keeps right on suffering.

Several years ago a genuine revival took place in a congregation
in southern Virginia. I, as a ministerial candidate, observed a
rare condition. People were laughing and crying simultaneously.
It was almost like heaven on earth. The community was excited.
Christians actually loved one another and expressed deep concern
for every individual. No person was left abandoned or destitute in
that community.

Years later, I became a minister of the gospel and returned to
conduct the funeral service of an aunt. This same congregation
was deader than the dead in the casket. Upon inquiring what had
transpired to lead to this tragic downfall, I was informed that the
deacons felt as though they had lost control of the church. Once these
deacons had reestablished their authority, the church instituted reform
which spelled out Icabod. Individuals suffered. Friendships were no
longer deep or dependable. The church had painted themselves into
a corner and failed to recognize the presence and power of the Holy
Spirit of God.

The crisis in our local assemblies has been met by another brother
who writes:

> "Overselling the church, pastors have found, is a
> mistake. While it's flattering to have new members,
> they're likely to become dragons and eventually do
> the church more harm than good if they come with
> an ideology that doesn't mesh with what's there. A
> small, cohesive family is better than a house divided,
> even a large house."[11]

One may question the reasoning in dwelling so much on the
established church when the targeted subject is isolation and
sequestering. Perhaps this illustration can shed some light on the
connection.

At one time, our family owned a bird dog that insisted on pointing
out field mice rather than quail. Although we were frustrated with his
apparent flaw, on a certain fall day in Carolina, this particular dog
suddenly stopped and pointed. It was, once again, what appeared to

be another false alarm when, sure enough; a quail was flushed. The dog's skill was genuine and the time spent proved to be fruitful even though it once seemed futile. This new bird dog had finally proved his point by the results of his indefatigable pursuit.

When pursuing the culprit in regards to loneliness, we often times find ourselves at the church door. This is not what we necessarily expect. We may expect consolation; we may discover dragons. We do not point at flaws in the church to simply criticize. The reason for this treatise is to call attention to our undoing as a body and dedicate ourselves to *be* the church, rather than simply attending one. "We have found the enemy," it has been said, "and it is us."

In dealing with the subject of pain, which is certainly experienced by those who are isolated, C.S. Lewis delivers words that serve to assist.

> "The dangers of apparent self-stuffiness explain why our Lord regards the vices of the feckless and dissipated so much more leniently than the vices that lead to worldly success. Prostitutes are in no danger of finding their present life so satisfactory that they cannot turn to God: the proud, the avaricious, the self-righteous, are all in that danger."[12]

The term doldrums, the condition being examined in this chapter, is best defined by Webster as a "gloomy, listless feeling with sluggishness or complete inactivity."[13] We could not have said it any better and that definition more than adequately defines the condition of those suffering from acute loneliness. We are living in a lonely society and there is certainly a lonely segment in our spiritual communities, as well. If we do not soon and suddenly discover our loss of godly community, we shall soon be consumed by lethargy and end up in a Laodicean ecumenicalism.

In order to cure the disease we must discover the cause. This is accomplished only by those willing to get their hands dirty, so to speak, by those willing to roll up their sleeves and thoroughly immerse themselves in a concerted effort to find solutions.

"God does not hide His hurt. He employs shocking language, comparing Israel to "a swift she-camel running here and there, a wild donkey accustomed to the desert, sniffing the wind in her craving - in her heat, who can restrain her? And that is the precise cycle of anger, grief, forgiveness, jealousy, love, pain that God Himself went through."[14]

In dealing with those who have been hurt or left alone to suffer, it also needs to be understood that God, at times, will allow such in order to develop one's character. Thus we, in our counseling, must allow provisions for growth and development during those periods of bewilderment. It must always be unmistakably clear that "whom the Lord loves He also chastens." God allowed biblical characters to face solitude, at times, in order to give them a special message and to make their *good* characters become the *best* of characters. We must allow time to produce the very best wine; may any judgmental folks please overlook this use of analogy. The gracious and good Horatio Bonar, a Scottish minister of the nineteenth century adds, "He (God) knows exactly what we need and how to supply it . . His training is no random work. It is carried out with exquisite skill."[15]

There are numerous individuals who have experienced, or who are experiencing, dreadful rejection which may result in isolation. When we have been rejected by family and friends we will more than likely avoid communication. Those rejected may become skittish about becoming too closely involved with others for fear that they will be wounded again. This is another inherent reason driving individuals to withdraw from society. Such hurting souls need competent counsel to overcome their fears and misgivings.

The biblical counselor has a decided advantage provided by the knowledge that the God of all creation was also rejected. He was rejected by family, friends and by those He came in love to redeem. When we fully understand this message, it gives us the utmost courage to continue. Rejection is most destructive and must be dealt with openly and thoroughly using the authority of the biblical account, which is supreme. Joseph would be an excellent example, being a type of our Lord Jesus Christ.

It has been the hand of God to lead me to an inspirational study of rejection. The book, by Charles Soloman, is a rich resource for those dealing with the subject, full of valuable thoughts and insights.

> "It is entirely possible for a person's behavior, once self has returned to the ascendancy, to be more defeated than before co-crucifixion became an appropriated reality. It is always good to remind ourselves as counselors and those with whom we share that self never changes from the time we were born until the time we die. Self or flesh is at enmity with God. It cannot be changed; it cannot be improved. The only proper place for it is death at the cross. Just as Freud and some of his successors have pointed out, all of the experiences of the past remain with us."[16]

Being a product of rejection and its many facets, experience in the field places me at a decided advantage, only in the sense that the experience has been governed by a thorough application of the scriptures. A case in point would be a passage found in Psalm 27:10, "When my father and my mother forsake me, then the Lord will take me up." While reading this you may become inquisitive, but suffice it to say; rejection is not foreign to this author. With this you should be encouraged in the certainty that, no matter what may be the trial, God will provide comfort and counsel and see His own to a safe harbor.

Legions of dear folk have suffered from all sorts of abuse which has led them to withdraw in seclusion. All these precious folk must be assisted by those of us who name the name of Christ. We must become dedicated to serious counsel. In doing so, we must not allow them to become dependent upon us, but dependent upon their Maker. Sometimes our empathy may weaken rather than strengthen a soul in distress.

> "Certain characteristics or behaviors enter into the definitions. For instance, one definition of codependency is: 'a psychological condition characterized by a preoccupation with another person

and his problems, hindering one's ability to develop healthy relationships with people.'"[17]

In counseling those afflicted by physical, mental, or emotional abuse there is a compelling need for counsel at the hand of the Almighty. We need to acquire by His leading the wisdom necessary to know the appropriate time to speak and the times we should remain silent. (Ecclesiastes 3:7). Sometimes silence is cowardice, while at other times, it is the leading of the Holy Spirit. It takes the leading of the Holy Spirit of God to know the appropriate responses that will bring help and healing to those lanquishing in loneliness. Some may wish to revert to their proverbial shells and never emerge. It takes patience, respect, and a humble dependency on the Holy Spirit to see, what may seem to be, painfully slow progress. Let us be vigilant and prayerful in our all-important dealings with those too long overlooked and shunned.

Man normally becomes anxious when left alone by others and especially when they feel left alone by God. Just when we need Him the most, in spite of the hymn that declares otherwise, He seems to have gone deaf or is too preoccupied to deal with our case. He is not there at that very moment we need Him, to comfort or cheer when we are destitute and lonely. What happened? What did we do wrong? A noted theologian steps up to help us in our perplexity.

> "He is not silent. The reason we have the answer is because the infinite - personal God, the full Trinitarian God, has not been silent. He has told us who He is. Couch your concept of inspiration and revelation in these terms, and you will see how it cuts down into the warp and woof of modern thinking. He is not silent. This is the reason we know. It is because He has spoken. What has He told us? Has He told us only about other things? No, He has told us true truth about Himself - that He is the infinite - personal God - we have the answer to existence."[18]

We may question. We may even wonder and ask why. Our Lord did so when He hung upon the cross. People from all ages and all walks of life have done so. Those left alone, who ask such questions, need not feel abandoned. They need to understand that when the wind stops blowing it by no means suggests that the wind is no longer in existence. There are times when we all need to be reminded of these latent truths. This is where the dedicated believer in Christ Jesus needs to arrive front and center. This is where well-versed biblical counselors can flex their spiritual muscles. Indeed, the Lord God Almighty is here in your plight and, as Schaeffer has reminded us, He is not silent.

There is a way out of the doldrums of this life which sometimes seems to engulf us in our desperation. Being alone when one is in need of intimacy can create consternation. It is at this moment we need to draw upon the encouragement of One who was acquainted with grief. "In the world you will have tribulation: but be of good cheer; I have overcome the world." (John 16:33). The comfort for the destitute is well grounded in that the Lord Himself faced periods of abandonment and we are not greater than He. Do not give up but give in to the One who understands more than you will ever comprehend.

> "The real Son of God is at your side. He is beginning to turn you into the same kind of thing as Himself. He's beginning, so to speak, to 'inject' His kind of life and thought, His zoe, into you; beginning to turn the tin soldier into a live man. The part of you that does not like it is the part that is still tin."[19]

So there you are. It is a facade. Its not reality after all. However, when it's happening to you, it does become real. And yet, as Lewis has declared, the Lord, at times, will allow bad things to take place in the lives of good folk in order to transform them into His image. The important thing, which must also be considered, is that when someone is in the midst of a solo flight; ground support is greatly welcomed.

Thus, in it all, we discover that the loneliness of man is something most people find exceedingly excruciating. They are often unwilling to admit their struggles or discuss their problems with others because of the fear they will not be understood or accepted. It is incumbent upon those of us who have been liberated from similar sequestering to be on the lookout for those who have fallen prey to this dreaded condition. Those who are redeemed cannot, they must not, allow those who are cast aside suffer needlessly, without hope. Godly individuals must not fail in their responsibility to provide assistance for those groping in discomfort. Do not hide in denial of what is transpiring in your world. We only pass this way once and we cannot recall nor revisit those magnificent opportunities once they are gone. These are opportunities set before us by the Almighty; we have been called to care.

"Denial puts off what should be faced. People in denial refuse to see loss for what it is, something terrible that cannot be reversed. They dodge pain rather than confront it. But their unwillingness to face pain comes at a price. Ultimately it diminishes the capacity of their souls to grow bigger in response to pain. They make the same mistake as patients who, following major surgery, refuse to get out of bed and put damaged muscles back to work. In the end denial leads to a greater loss."[20]

Failure to assist those who are in pain, whether physical or emotional, is inhumane and ultimately shall meet with judgment. For echoing down through the corridors of history, one can hear the voice of Jesus declaring; "Inasmuch as you have done it unto the least of these my brethren, you have done it unto me." (Matthew 25:40).

CHAPTER FIVE

Devoted to a Credible Solution

The silence is deafening! There is a silence that, at times, is most welcome. However, when silence serves only to fuels one's misery; it is most unwelcome. We are anxious to provide comfort to any and all who are suffering in their very silent worlds due to the lack of kinship in this hurry-up, preoccupied society.

It is essential to provide a means of egress to those who have become smothered by their loneliness and consequent solitude. One must be carefully guided out of darkness into light, out of their doldrums into a life of devotion discovered in the greatest of Liberators. A devoted and gifted counselor that uses proper biblical means to extricate the sequestered is a God-send. Therefore, we are now moving into a phase of biblical therapy which may ultimately be the salvation of those who are ostracized in their empty world of loneliness. We shall move on prayerfully and confidently under the leading of His counsel.

In the study of this condition it is evident that we are dealing with a phase of emotional distress which has been overlooked or misunderstood by most. In previous chapters, we have seen the effects of isolation from personal experience and have cited Christ's familiarity with the heartache of solitude and rejection. In this chapter, we shall consider the removal of this obstacle by means of dedicated, loyal and devoted extrication. In order to be truly effective in assisting the sequestered soul, we must allow ourselves to become fully acquainted with this ordeal. Consider walking a mile in someone else's shoes. Have you ever walked through a park and seen families picnicking, children laughing and playing, only to spot a person sitting all alone on a cold park bench? Did you ever ask yourself, "Could they use a friend?" Have you ever been to a restaurant with family or friends and noticed the uneasiness of a person left to eat all by themselves?

> "No one feels lonelier than a depressed person at a party. I suspect half the congregation feels every Sunday morning what Naomi felt when she arrived in Bethlehem. When a friend tells you he is so excited about all that God is doing, its hard to admit you're irritated over what God is not doing."[1]

With this information we must incorporate the subject at hand which, of course, is that of being left alone and destitute. There is no pain quite equal to that of feeling that you are a motherless child, that you are all alone in a dark and uncaring world with no comfort or security on the horizon. That is the explicit reason behind this section in dealing with an individual's plight, that you may embrace with complete devotion their rescue and emancipation from this pitfall.

Such a calamity will need devotion on the part of both counselor and counselee. All of our expertise derived from the former chapters must now be exercised fully through prayer and genuine loyalty to each other to slay the dragon that is all-consuming. Only those who have completely lost their breath or have come face to face with a life threatening situation can fully appreciate that feeling of desperation. Those who have fallen prey to loneliness can testify that they may have wept so frequently that they no longer care to cry. It becomes

like dry heaves in this ongoing grief. One visits a church expecti
to discover someone or something for consolation and, oftentimes,
they are sorely disillusioned. It is then that a voice within reminds us
to cast ourselves upon the Lord and He shall surely sustain us.

In one's desperation it becomes comforting to come to the place
where one's deepest frustrations are met with His silent assurance
that He has been where they now are. Somehow, as one casts himself
at the feet of Jesus he discovers the wounds which testify of His deep
association with rejection. Christ stood alone, at times, with regard
to family and friends who failed to be there for Him in His times
of desperation. It is at this point in time that, somehow, tranquility
defeats terrible emptiness.

> "We forsake Him by seeking to please ourselves
> for a time and agreeing to take Him later. Forsaking
> God, thinking of self. Prairie dwellers seeing fire
> approaching, burn off a space and gather themselves
> together in the space burned off. As the wind drives
> the furious fire it reaches the burned space, it travels
> around them and they are saved. Christ is the burned
> space in which we are saved."[2]

The yielding to our Lord in time of utter loneliness is sometimes
sheer surrender. We believe that we are at the very bottom of a dark
and cold shaft and are really at our wit's end. And immediately, in
our desperation, we gain strength in stories such as that of the widow
in II Kings 4. She had come to the end of herself. Her containers for
sustenance had run dry. She was called upon to present her empty
vessels in faith and miraculously they were filled! The oil supply only
stopped because of a lack of containers to fill! Our supply is unlimited
when we, in faith, turn to Him who can supply all of our needs. We
bring our empty and barren lives to be filled by His renewing and
energizing Spirit. What a bountiful supply!

Do you encounter God in your circumstances? Then do you want
to experience true happiness? Submit yourself peacefully and simply
to the will of God and bear your sufferings without struggle, as some
have suggested.

"As wonderful as this sounds, it still may not stop you from bargaining with God. The hardest thing about suffering is not knowing how great it will be or how long it will last. You will be tempted to want to impose some limits to your suffering. No doubt you will want to control the intensity of the pain."[3]

In their desperation, the believer can discover a solace in their ultimate devotion to Him who can completely comprehend , by personal experience, their distress. We need to be reminded that our Maker also was a man of sorrows and was fully acquainted with human grief.

Upon a thorough study of the Canticles, one who is desperate will certainly come to the best of terms with the Lover of their souls. Indeed, there are times when the bridegroom seems to be playing "hide and go seek" with the bride. And yet, in the final analysis, they join in harmony and unite in an unending love affair where loneliness gives way to lavishness.

Thus in one's search, there is a discovery of a genuine loyalty and a deep affection for the One who draws them with unsearchable devotion. Meanwhile, in the journey of life, we, like in Pilgrim's Progress, meet with both friend and foe. When challenged by our solo stance in our venture we may consider the utter agony Christ suffered in the abandonment and betrayal of His friends. This is the very crux of the thesis. And it is here where we either go under or we survive. Will we be open to the Spirit's leading in facing our dilemma and bow in submission to our Creator? Enter now the unique and gifted biblical counselor. In order to liberate an individual from this painful sequestering the cause must be established. There is a cure but; we must first understand the illness.

After traversing this distance it becomes apparent that one who suffers such a malady requires a source beyond themselves. Once the cause is determined then the cure is in the determination to persevere in conquering the unseen enemy. This enemy will crop up in every facet of life and you must become educated in his devices.

"Loneliness is the running theme among pastor's wives, the piper's tune that drives them online. 'What do you think is the No. 1 problem that the preacher's wives have?' says Lynne Dugan, author of *Heart to Heart With Pastor's Wives.* Friendship. Loneliness. You're surrounded by these other people in the congregation, and you feel isolated."[4]

And there you have it, hot off the press. April 2007. The unaddressed emotional conflict now begins to emerge. A beneficial aspect of this is that we see, on the surface, the reason for the feelings of alienation in this particular group of individuals. Again, if such is not taken seriously it may result into a deeper emotional upheaval and could ultimately lead to divorce. Such sequestered souls need not resort to going online but need to be led to strong bible based counsel in order to overcome the unrelenting enemy.

Our God is glorified when His servants undergo severe conflicts and emerge victorious. However, when we become more satisfied with our accomplishments than in dealing with the agonies of life; we miss His best for us. These are times when we may become deprived of what we know as happiness in order to experience a deeper joy.

An article in the local paper, taken from the Washington Post and written by Shankar Vedantam has come to my attention. Underlying this article may well be the very subject matter which now occupies our attention. "About one in four people diagnosed with depression are actually reacting normally to stressful events like divorce or losing a job, according to a new study."[5] Mr. Vedantam continues to elaborate in his findings which may well support my hypothesis relative to some of the matters being dealt with in this thesis.

> "The finding could have far-reaching consequence for the diagnosis of depression, the growing use of symptom checklists in identifying people who might be depressed and the $12 billion a year U.S. market for antidepressant drugs. Patients are currently diagnosed on the basis of a constellation of symptoms that include sadness, fatigue and suicidal thoughts. The diagnostic manual used by psychiatrists says that anyone who suffers from at least five such symptoms for as little as two weeks may be clinically depressed."[6]

With such an insidious topic as socio-spiritual sequestering, or loneliness, it is essential that we delve deeper into the reasons behind depression, such as sadness, fatigue, suicide or even the helpless feeling of ostracism. Again, such delicate matters need the attention of society. But in most cases it is overlooked until one seeks advice or counseling. It may be astounding to discover just how many souls there are who have fallen subject to this hideous onslaught plaguing humanity. This gives merit and credence to the tireless pursuit of solutions for those suffering under the weight of such diabolical heaviness. Our solid commitment to honor God is our service to others must not waver.

One's devotion to God and the desire to become liberated is the only genuine means of solace. No matter the extenuating circumstance, the ultimate goal must always be found in the One who knows you and how to bring healing into your situation. This may require a third party who is spiritually qualified to guide you to a safe harbor and consolation in the Master. But those who fail or refuse to recognize this blight in life do not understand how serious a matter it is that confronts us. Upon following this treatise closely one must be all but convinced that this point is most valid. Thus, in the spiritual body there must be that monovalent therapy that brings divine healing to those afflicted.

> "Frieda Fromm-Reichmann noted that at least one reason we have no very good theory about loneliness is that we have studied it so little. She suggested that the absence of attention to loneliness was to be expected not by the challenge loneliness presented to understanding but rather by the threat it presented to well-being. She said that loneliness is 'such a painful, frightening experience that people will do practically everything to avoid it.'"[7]

This information certainly supports our recent remarks in particular and the entire thesis in general. Again, still another author has become acquainted with the matter at hand. Little by little data accumulates that gives impetus to this theme of the lonely heart. Only when we fully appreciate such studies and information do we come to the realization that an emotion is running wild in our society which must become a part of our psychological manual. Loneliness must never be trivialized by counselors and certainly not by biblical counselors who have the heart and mind of Christ.

> "One of the difficulties with loneliness is that it becomes so overpowering with its influence, emotional gloom, physical disability, and mental sluggishness that you find it more and more difficult to escape - unless you make a concentrated effort."[8]

As we delve into other's writings we observe that there are those who, also, have become increasingly aware of this shadow in the twilight. They acknowledge that the condition has either gone undetected or has been ignored. However, the more research grows the more awareness there is of the stranglehold loneliness has on our society. If you have never been there you must consider yourself most fortunate. But for the most part , those who are honest and forthright will testify that desperation has visited their lives at one point or another. Not all bouts with loneliness are of a prolonged nature, but those who have dealt for short periods with the anguish of isolation must certainly empathize with those who have endured chronic loneliness.

Recently a group met in a local restaurant after a preaching service. One lady was eating by herself and without hesitation yours truly approached her with words of cheer. She related that her husband was out of town but she was most appreciative of being noticed and thankful for words of consolation. This was no special service, granted, however it does indicate that this matter is taken personally and seriously. Those who have personal dealings with afflictions in the lives of others are usually more apt to be alert and responsive to what may, otherwise, go unnoticed by many. You, dear reader, may or may not have had bouts with isolation, sequestering or such emotional upheaval and this is the reason for this chronicle. Then, too, it may serve to assist you later in life's journey as you review this journal and gain inspiration from its contents.

Experience proves to be one of our best instructors. As we learn from what transpires in our lives and the lives of others we are able to differentiate between being alone and being lonely.

> "Being alone without the explicit condition of loneliness is an act of conscious control, volition, thought and determination. Being alone is necessary pause, being lonely is an ultimate condition. Being alone implies an evolution or continuity of experience, while being lonely means a total, radical change. Being alone is a way back to others. Being lonely is a way back to oneself."[9]

This probably needs no explanation; however, let's delve a bit deeper on "being lonely is a way back to oneself." Here is where the rubber meets the road, so to speak. This becomes the focal point with relation to our study of the subject at hand.

When one is afflicted with lonesomeness, that precious human being needs helpful therapy. It is at this very juncture that those who understand the problem may be best equipped to bring consolation and liberation to the wounded. Unfortunately, in all too many areas, we are not there for those who are desperate. Then, in all cases, the only real prescription is that of utter devotion on the part of both the counselee and the counselor. And, "a friend loves at all times." (Proverbs 17:17). So then believer, it is our duty and privilege to guide the bewildered to emancipation. This liberation is most successful when the para-humanitarian will stop being pious and will get down to where one is actually hurting. Join in the fight and weep with those who weep. Empathize all the while in your counsel, urging their devotion to Him who, alone, can free the slave from self and sorrow.

Most of us like to hold little ones in our arms, especially when you can return them to their parents on short notice. But we are more prone to hold them close to us when they have been bathed, well powdered, etc. Please do not present me with one that needs some serious attention. Likewise, when we come upon one in distress and drowning in grief we must not hand them back to another. Do more than quote your favorite scripture verse and send them on their "merry way." We, as believers, are to put ourselves in their place and offer assistance. If we are unsuccessful in freeing them, we may look to others who may further assist, but we should stay involved and available.

Devotion to Jesus always becomes the very best antidote to all who have become sequestered. There are many ways for cure, as there are many ways to God, but Christ is ultimately the way to God and the way for our healing, as well.

> "Immanuel means we don't have to feel alone. There is an aloneness that comes even in the midst of a large crowd of people - just ask any young child who has ever been lost in a crowd. There is the aloneness of being misunderstood. There is the aloneness of being in an empty house or apartment, all by oneself, night after night. And there is the aloneness of trying to carry a heavy load without help."[10]

If you have read thus far and have not been moved physically, spiritually, and emotionally you need to put this down and seek some serious instruction. Some years ago, while in college, a student wondered if his professor always read those lengthy reports he had to submit. In one report of great length he placed in the middle of the contents, "If you get this far, I'll buy you ice cream." The report was graded and returned to the young seminarian. At the end of the paper the professor wrote, "Make mine chocolate." It will not be necessary for you to report but it would be most gratifying to learn that you have met with some blessed thought provoking information throughout this study.

As we continue to accumulate more information buried in books, papers, periodicals, etc. we discover the importance of the subject together with the dearth of informative materials and research. However, what has been unearthed has vastly contributed to our study of people who have become entangled in the maze, i.e., those who have found themselves in a socio-sequestered world. And what a challenge to be able to express one's deepest and innermost thoughts in regard to providing a credible means of assistance through the door of ultimate devotion in Christ our Lord.

In our examination of this field we know as loneliness, there is an area which we may need to consider. There are those who often resent the memories of former days or occasions that are now illusive. Recalling such events can lead to pronounced agony ending in a withdrawal or seclusion. This is most disconcerting and can be the worst of all ventures, without question.

> "Memories were, and are, beautiful to me. I cling to them as a man clings to a plank of wood while lost in the middle of the sea. But they are also troubling because they are only that- memories. They are vestiges of a past I will never again possess. They involve people I will never see. I cannot live with memories, and I cannot live without them."[11]

O yes, you can't live with 'em and you can't live without 'em. Ever heard that before? True. But when it comes to holding on to past memories in an unhealthy manner, we must discover something to replace those thoughts.

First, it may be in one's best interest to discard things such as clothing or personal effects once owned by a friend or loved one. This is exceedingly difficult to accomplish, however, in the long run it may be a part of the healing process. Try to think of it as your contribution to one who may be in need of those items. At the same time, you may wish to introduce some new and different keepsakes or furnishings into your domicile. Possibly, if you are a neatnik and do not want to clean up after a newly acquired pet, you might consider shopping for an aquarium. At any rate, you need to make some adjustments in your own way, manner, and in your own time frame. No one can do what you can and in the manner which you wish for it to be accomplished. A word of caution, if you are suffering from the loss of a mate *do not*, let it be reiterated, *do not* make any hurried or rash decisions. Folks who are lonely may resort to selling their prized possessions, a home, or whatever in haste and sooner or later regret it and are unable to revert to their original circumstances and lifetime accumulations. Then it is too late!

There are those memories which one may never dismiss. Some good and some not so good. Personally it is my contention that those who have lost a mate or exceedingly precious person in life need to keep going forward and hesitate to reflect too much on the past. Memories are illusive. In trying to relive the past we grow melancholy and become weak and thwarted in our present and future lives. Nothing can become more disconcerting for the lonely as to constantly look back and long for those "good ole days." Revisit, of course, but to constantly revert to those yesteryear events may well lead to one's getting "stuck" in the past, making it hard for them to truly appreciate the present.

Those who have become excessively lonely may best lose themselves in a section of God's love letter that is the ultimate in comfort and closeness. When one is overwhelmed, when the fires are all consuming, the waters are swift and deep; they need to go to the Rock. There they may be lifted above all the consuming elements which are most devastating and destructive, including the enemy of loneliness with which we do battle.

> "How do we quiet our hearts long enough to listen to our tumultuous emotions? We can start by hearing the divinely inspired words of those who provide us with glimpses into inner worlds. No section of the Bible teaches us the language of the soul better than the Psalms, which reflect the movement of the human heart in rich, evocative and startling language. In a voice that disrupts, invites and reveals, the psalmist draws us to the voice of God."[12]

Time and space prohibits a study of the Psalms, however, it must be included in this study as a medication for those in desperation. Therefore, just a sampling of this marvelous collection will whet the appetite of those who have become isolated and despondent. Return to the Psalms to find the answer to the soul's inexplicable thirst.

Here are some excerpts from that account which will aid our search for a lasting peace. Psalm 4:8, "I will lay me down in peace and sleep: for you Lord only make me dwell in safety." Then again, there is Psalm 16:7, "I will bless the Lord, who has given me counsel: my reins also instruct me in the night seasons." What about Psalm 18:35 where we learn that God's gentleness with us is that which has caused us to become really great? Psalm 23 is known best by most: including Protestants, Jews, and Roman Catholics. It provides the best source of medication when read, by the lonely especially, morning, noon and night for seven days in succession. (Only take this medication as prescribed in that last phrase.)

This book is replete with consolation for the lost, the longing, and yes, the lonely. If you, like this author, do not have the benefit of being brought up by your biological parents, there is a passage in Psalm 27:10. "When my father and mother forsake me, then the Lord will take me up." It has become, however, this man's experience to have been adopted by others and by the Almighty, Himself. So go on now, and make some discoveries on your own in this magnificent chronicle. Take it personally for indeed it was written with that very thought in mind.

In this examination of the socio-spiritually sequestered, it has taken us from detachment, to becoming disturbed, desperate with certain doldrums to this portion which deals with one's devotedness to their God and Maker. Devotedness to God is most vital and is the means by which one may be extricated from their dilemma.

This word, "devoted," is described in the dictionary as "dedicated, consecrated, loving, loyal or faithful."[13] Beloved, that really captures my innermost feelings at this juncture. Unless one exercises all of the above they may well be sequestered eternally. The affected soul must become completely absorbed in freedom from the enemy which requires dedication. It will require your concerted effort and loving loyalty to your Creator. Furthermore, there must be total faithfulness in all this emancipation. It has come to my attention that the best acronym for faith is: Forsaking All I Trust Him. Right on!

We humans will, at times, revert to our former lifestyles with regard to our emotions and deep seated feelings. It is vital to keep open to the things of God and, if possible, commit to memory some passages surrounding the theme of loneliness and isolation, which may return in our weaker moments. Such passages to be considered have been suggested by Gary Collins, a Christian counselor. On page thirty three his book entitled, *Effective Counseling*, he lists Psalm 27:10, Proverbs 18:24, John 15:14, and Hebrews 13:5. Interestingly enough, we have in some manner addressed all these with the exception of the passage in Hebrews which reads, "I will never leave you, nor forsake you." This is a good addition to the other scriptures we have called attention to in this treatise. Just understand that we must not be discouraged in a relapse but we must institute a means of escape. This is where one does well to have intimate friendships; people who are Bible based and alert to your misgivings and shortcomings. The greatest trapeze artists, who love life, systematically resort to a safety net. A wise philosopher left us this old adage, "an ounce of prevention is worth a pound of cure."

In our devotion to our Maker and Lord we express our deepest feelings in that lost art we know as worship. The reason we refer to worship as a lost art is due to the fact that many in our age do not understand nor do they engage in the style of worship that God has designed and welcomes. The lonely, the sequestered, and all those in between, find the very greatest means of exodus is in spirit filled worship of Almighty God.

> "In considering the rationale for God-centered worship, we must begin with the realization that worship is the number one priority of the Church. Jesus' famous statement in John 4:23 that the Father seeks worshipers is unparalleled, for no where in the entire corpus of Holy Scripture do we read of God's seeking anything else from a child of God. God desires worship above all else."[14]

We must, also, understand that even God in all His marvelous attributes lays Himself bare in His dealings with humanity. In many or most cases those who become isolated and often are found hurting will do whatever it takes to hide their tears and their deepest feelings of betrayal. It is imperative that such individuals understand that we have a God with personal, human experience in every area that we may encounter.

Getting angry is not a sin, for we know that there are things that make God angry. We may get angry, but it must not lead us to sin, and we are not to let the sun go down with anger remaining in us. Nevertheless, the lonely have a legitimate and a deep seated need, at certain times, to express their anger due to their ill treatment by some unkind bystanders. There is no excuse for friends or family to neglect the needy or to allow those who become withdrawn to go on suffering without others displaying compassion. Again, there are others who will speak cruelly about a person who they have falsely accused of being a weird hermit of sorts. The book of James does an excellent job in dealing with a loose tongue. There is a humorous tale related by Kent Hughes with his recollection of John Wesley, the father of Methodism. "Mr. Wesley, the strings on your tie are much too long. (A female congregant remarked). It's offensive to me!"[15] Mr. Wesley then asked if any of the ladies happened to carry scissors in their purses. When he was given scissors he then gave them to the woman who had complained. She proceeded to cut the strings clear up to the preacher's collar. Wesley asked her if she was satisfied and she said it was much improved. It was then that the evangelist spoke these words to the woman. "I'm sure you wouldn't mind if I also gave you a bit of correction. I must tell you, madam, that your tongue is an offense to me - it's too long! Please stick it out . . I'd like to take some off."[16]

Folks can be just as mean as a reptile and their venom even more injurious to those already afflicted. If this remark may seem a bit too caustic then be observant of the "Sweet Psalmist of Israel," the man after God's own heart, and read some of his writings. David feared only God and never man. And so we speak to any and all who come down hard on the afflicted. If you are the subject of a sharp tongue of criticism, then you may find yourself in the most excellent company of kings and prophets.

It occurred to me that perhaps the most beneficial portion of Holy Writ for the subject at hand may be found in Matthew's gospel, chapter five. The beatitudes cover the matter of such bewilderment completely. Actually, the first and second beatitudes are all-inclusive. "Blessed are the poor in spirit," and "Blessed are they that mourn" speak to the soul of loneliness like nothing else. These dear souls are fully acquainted with both the need and He who supplies. Herein lies our comfort, for certain. Jesus Christ knew our need long before our sequestering took place, therefore, He has provided us with the antidote for such in these marvelous writings. Take it from one who knows from personal experience, dear one; there is hope for blessed deliverance from your warfare.

Within the pages of *The New Rebellion Handbook,* there are the top ten indicators of the Spirit's activity in your life. Let us select from these a few to bring aid to your situation.

> "You feel an unexplainable peace in the midst of stressful circumstances. You sense God's nearness and comfort when you are grieving. Your appetite for God's Word gets stronger and stronger. You long to spend time with God and be in His presence. You find it unexpectedly easier to be patient and kind."[17]

We are now beginning to develop a metamorphic transition from being a worm in loneliness to a butterfly in loveliness. We now arrive at the threshold of being devotees of all that leads to total liberation from darkness through His tender care. In our transformation we look to see from whence it originated to where we now find ourselves.

Whether in the life of the one liberated from dreaded isolationism or for one who may serve as a type of midwife in delivering the afflicted, we take heart and rejoice in this liberation. Then, too, once freed of this ugly, unwanted demonic plague, we are to guard against back-sliding into it's jaws. Remember to stay close to the Liberator, surround yourself with godly friends and counsel and do not look back.

> "We live a time secure; beloved and loving, sure it cannot last for long, then the goodbyes come - again like a small death, the closing of a door. One learns to live with the pain. One looks ahead, not back never back, only before. And joy will come again warm and secure, if only for the now, laughing, we endure.[18]

Do you recall what happened to Lot's wife when she looked back? We are told that as she looked back at Sodom and Gomorrah she turned into a pillar of salt. A young lad who heard this story in his Sunday School class remarked, "Aw, that's nothin'. My Mom was driving, looked back and turned into a telephone pole!" The focus is on the "not turning back" part. When we look back we will often yield the same results as Lot's wife or the dear mother at the wheel.

It seems I recall something else about looking back from the lips of our Chief Counselor in Luke 9:62. "No man, having put his hand to the plough and looks back, is fit for the kingdom of God." Somehow, my faithful reader, it seems that you may now have no need for such weighty admonition as you have hopefully found His way out of your circumstances.

EPILOGUE

As we journey through life we constantly discover things, about our world, that are new to us. This has been especially true for me in regard to the field of medicine and disease. For instance, I recently learned of a medical condition known as Asperger's Syndrome. I found out about the disease through a teenager who is stricken with the disorder. She is a precious gift from God and it would not surprise me if I have learned more from her than she has learned from me. I have nicknamed her "Butterfly" because of her spirit and beauty.

Another friend, that I met recently in my journey for the Master, has yet another condition that was unfamiliar to me when we first met. This individual has what is referred to as Reflex Sympathetic Dystrophy Syndrome, or RSDS. It is interesting that such a disease may be used here to illustrate the emotional disease we have been dealing with our study of the socio-spiritually sequestered. The effects of RSDS go virtually unnoticed by the general public. It is not readily apparent to the onlooker that the affected individual is in distress; just as many Christians cannot detect those who are socio-spiritually afflicted, nor can they appreciate their pain. Most physicians have no clue as to the agony of the RSDS sufferer and treatments so far have proven most ineffective. Those afflicted with this condition may look as healthy as a professional athlete, but this is definitely not the case. Those who suffer the wrenching distress of loneliness may not display outward signs indicating an inner turmoil, however, their agony is no less authentic. The fact that loneliness is often an unseen or "invisible" condition, is the very reason why we are sounding the alarm so urgently; this sequestering must be exposed.

During the writing of this epilogue, I had the privilege of meeting an Iranian gentleman at a nearby mall. With tears in his eyes he told me how lonely he felt, especially at night, being all by himself. He would have never related this information to me, had he not heard I was researching this theme for my dissertation. How many others are there in our communities who are craving meaningful companionship?

While pondering the subject, that is at the heart of our current topic, the prophet, Ezekiel, came to mind, ready to take center stage. Although his message was declared thousands of years ago, the relevancy to our discussion is undeniable.

The message of Ezekiel that deserves our attention is found in Ezekiel 33:6. Caution is at the core of this worthy watchman's pronouncement. "And if," Ezekiel reports, "the watchman see the sword come, and blow not the trumpet, and the people be not warned; if the sword come, and take any person from among them, he is taken away in his iniquity; but his blood will I require at the watchman's hand."

How exceedingly easy to become instructed by our Creator as to the necessity of telling the truth, the whole truth, and nothing but the truth. This is applicable not just for settling conflicts of our judicial system; it is of relevance in our dealing with the crisis of those who are lost and lonely. This passage continues by pointing out that "if we warn the wicked of his way to turn from it; if he does not turn from his way, he shall die in his iniquity; but you have delivered your soul." (vs. 9)

The message rings clear and plain for those of us desiring to serve our needy society. If those of us who study the matter at hand fail to sound the alarm, then we are seriously at fault. Then again, we are reminded by the Apostle Paul of still another conflict. "For if the trumpet gives an uncertain sound, who shall prepare himself for battle?" (I Corinthians 14:8.) This, of course, brings us back to our original suggestion to "tell it like is" so others will rally to the critical cause of rescuing the disenfranchised among us.

It is not what happens *to* you and me that matters; it is what happens *in* us that counts. The enemy and his cohorts are devious in the way in which they swallow up anybody and everybody who drifts along with the current. We are living in the best of days and the worst of days. People have access to godly information and instruction unlike people who lived just decades ago. At the same time, there is more confusion and heartache in our day due to the failure of God's people to meet the dire, unseen needs in the lives of those who have been left behind, so to speak.

After reflecting on the contents of this vital subject it has occurred to me what may be the answer to much of our failure to respond to the many who need our attention.

There is a desperate need for a spiritual revival. A revival is, according to the dictionary, "a stirring up of religious faith among those who have been indifferent ; profession of renewed faith."[1] Revivals are usually orchestrated by church leaders. However, there are few of any consequence transpiring today. Understand, we are not speaking in terms of evangelism or evangelistic meetings, but revival, or a "bringing back into use." Evangelistic meetings are primarily a means of reaching the unsaved with the gospel, whereas revival is bringing saved people back to proper devotion to Christ the Lord.

In Psalm 85:6, the psalmist has stolen my thunder! "Will you not revive us again that your people may rejoice in you?" Yes! When do you witness a Holy Ghost, God ordained revival, if ever? Churches may advertise that they are going to have revival which is not only presumptuous but, often, dishonest. Some of our churches are reaching out to the unsaved and people are coming to Christ. But even in our evangelism there is much room for improvement. Some of our churches are growing in membership but quantity does not always translate to quality. Becoming a member of a church does not predispose a person to devotion or committed service to Christ. Revival among God's people seems woefully lacking.

God would glory in sending a revival but there is a matter which is hindering His hand. The logjam restricting the flow of God's outpouring is a coldness among His flock, a disobedience to His greatest commandment, to love God and to love one's neighbor. The measure of our love for God may be reflected by hurried and insincere worship. The measure of our love for neighbors may be reflected in our hurried and insincere fellowship with others.

One of the greatest evangelists of all time stated that there would be no need of his services if churches had been carrying out their responsibilities. There would be no need for a revivalist if the church was, in our day, loving God with all their heart, soul and strength and loving their neighbor as Christ loves the Church. The call for revival is a call to love God in genuine worship and to love one another with the unabashed servant's heart. There is no need for people to feel isolated in the community of Christ.

Do you recall the Welsh revivals in 1904? There were no arrests made during the entire year. Amazing results. People were closer in their relationships in all this outpouring of the Spirit. There was a Great Awakening with Timothy Dwight, president of Yale University, who was inspired to pen the hymn, "I Love Thy Kingdom, Lord." All such outpourings created an atmosphere which dispelled despair and created warmth among the people of God in His church.

Loneliness among millions may soon be quelled with a warm spirit of revival in our land. We are not experiencing revival because we quench His Spirit by demanding control. Man must not seek to control God's people, God's church, or God's Spirit. We are experts at organizing committees for every possible project. We often boast of our accomplishments and programs, but we need to determine if what we are doing is the actual work that Christ has called us to do. Someone has remarked that a camel is a horse put together by a committee!

There may be a Jezebel spirit at work in our midst. Again, this is a spirit of control. Jezebel was in control of Ahab and all the kingdom. In Revelation 2:18 she reappears in a church in Thyatira and she is alive and well in many of our churches in 2007. It is a spirit of control which stifles the life and liberty of sequestered folk. By the way, ten million Hebrews left their places of worship to follow Baal and only seven thousand remained true to Almighty God. What does that tell you about where we really are today? We wonder why dear folk are depressed and feel betrayed as we go on, leaving them to fend for themselves. Instead of binding up their wounds, we often add insult to injury.

Please keep this information before you. The greatest reformer of all time did not leave his church, the church left him. However, what is needed today is not a reformation but a transformation. The church of Christ has so much baggage that she is no longer properly equipped to meet the longings of the lonely. As Nehemiah reported from his experience with Judah, "There is much rubbish, so that we are not able to build the wall." (Nehemiah 4:10.) There is too much that is of no significance today in the church and a revival is unable to thrive is such an environment.

Most conservative theologians are in agreement that the return of our Lord is most imminent and evangelicals in all walks concur. However, we seem to have forgotten what proceeds the rapture of the Church and the Second Coming, which are described in I Thessalonians 4:16,17 and I Thessalonians 3:13. Yes, the apostasy, which is mentioned in II Thessalonians 2:3. Jesus questioned, "When I return can I expect to see faith on the earth?" (Luke 18:8.) Therefore, we must be living on the perimeter of the great apostasy. All who are longing for genuine community, or koinonia, have become sorely frustrated.

With all this information before us, it is fitting for us to examine the state of the Church. Is not one of the prime reasons that we have vast numbers of lonely, disconnected individuals in our churches due to the fact that we are reaping what we have sown? It is with fervor that this treatise has been labored over for our consideration. But may it not be just for our consideration but may it spur us to become involved with those who, like the many I have interviewed, are out there awaiting our embrace.

If this discussion fails to arouse you then you need to drop to your knees and plead for a vision. Somehow, I believe that the impact of this subject will spark a flame in you that the Spirit of God will fan into a raging inferno bringing light and warmth to the sequestered soul.

The sequestered, under most conditions, will not manifest their innermost trepidations. Therefore, we are dependent upon the Holy Spirit of God to speak to our hearts, our minds, and our very spirits when we are dealing with the desperate individual. If we are receptive to His Spirit, God may divulge information that may not be apparent or observable under normal circumstances. This requires a yielded vessel. God does not seek counselors interested in self-promotion, but servants devoted to assisting and inspiring those who have lost hope. The biblical counselor who fails to meet these criteria should exit the counseling field forth-with.

With regard to those who are desperate, we who have the wisdom of God need, also, to assume precautionary measures. There are those who will "carry a tin cup" in hopes of receiving "coins of sympathy" from the gullible. A word of caution is in order at this juncture. This is certainly not intended to discourage us from carrying out our responsibilities before God. We should never become maliciously judgmental or critical, but we are admonished to be fruit examiners. Our Lord cautioned us in Matthew 7:16, "You shall know them by their fruits." Those who are genuine in their circumstances should prove to be open and sincere in their dealings with those who have been called to serve them.

Within the content of this book there may emerge those who have differing opinions in regard to some controversial subjects. It becomes evident to this writer that, indeed, I have made some statements that do not coincide with positions I formerly held. However, in dealing on a personal basis with pastors, professors, counselors and counselees, my views have shifted considerably. If you will walk and talk with the lonely and the desolate, perhaps the opinions I have shared will come into clearer focus. If ideas that have been shared are new ideas to you, consider them carefully before rushing to judgment. Our minds, like parachutes, are only useful when open. There are other authors who have had seasons of despair and have walked with forsaken souls who have proven themselves with credentials far beyond this author. Perhaps their wisdom in such matters will prove beneficial. Consider this advice from Dr. Billy Graham.

"When we criticize, act unkindly, belittle the work of others by careless or unappreciative words, we smother the fire and put it out. This happens many times when there is a fresh, new, or different movement of the Spirit of God - perhaps not using the old traditional methods in proclamation or service. For example, when some Christians sometimes seek to block what God may be doing in a new way."[2]

Another, more recent quote is taken from the writings of George Barna, president of Barna Research.

"We must be very careful how we critique another person's spiritual journey. If someone's path conforms to biblical guidelines - even though they stray from church traditions, cultural expectations, or our personal comfort zone - we must accept the possibility that God may be working through him or her in a manner that is different from how he is working through us, or perhaps different from the ways we have previously seen or experienced his leading. We are called to be wise and discerning but not judgmental."[3]

As we arrive at the end of this most provocative subject, it must be understood that there is no end to what this provocative subject incorporates. Sometime ago, I witnessed a film depicting the life of a famous gentleman of high regard. The movie ended in a most unique manner. Rather than the usual words "The End" at the conclusion, the words "The Beginning" appeared at the close of the film. The message was obvious and it let the audience know that even though the man's life had come to an end, his work would continue. We are reminded that the end of this life is merely the beginning of a much better life for the believer.

This, certainly, does not end with this informative instruction. It is the launching of essential acts of mercy to all who are in need of something better in their lives, and for the multitudes in distress around them. Look about you and examine your own set of circumstances. Determine for yourself what is essential in combating this modern day epidemic, this escalation of socio-spiritually sequestered individuals. If you have found yourself in the pages of this writing, may you find answers herein. For those who have been emboldened to enter the fray, may God give you the grace to break down strongholds in His name, providing deliverance for the captive for His eternal glory. Thus you become a part of this ongoing warfare and indeed, this is not the end of the story, it is really...

THE BEGINNING

Notes

PROLOGUE

1. John Eldridge, *Epic* (Nashville, Tennessee: Thomas Nelson, Inc., 2004), 23.

2. Larry Crabb, *Shattered Dreams* (Colorado Springs, Colorado: Waterbrook Press, 2005), 2.

3. David Wilkerson, *Suicide* (Lindale, Texas: David Wilkerson Publications, 1978), 101.

4. Granger E. Westberg, *Good Grief* (Philadelphia, Pennsylvania: Fortress Press, 1962), 28.

CHAPTER ONE: DETACHED

1. Andrew D. Lester, *It Hurts So Bad, Lord!* (Nashville, Tennessee: Broadman Press, 1976), 86.

2. Dr. James Dobson, *When God Doesn't Make Sense* (Wheaton, Illinois: Tyndale House Publishers, Inc., 1993), 18.

3. Randy Alcorn, *Heaven* (Wheaton, Illinois: Tyndale House Publishers, 2004), 120.

4. Max Lucado, *On The Anvil,* (Wheaton, Illinois: Tyndale House Publishers, 1985), 38.

5. *Facts and Trends* Vol. 53, No. 2 (March/April, 2007), 10.

6. Granger E. Westberg, *Good Grief* (Philadelphia, Pennsylvania: Fortress Press, 1962), 29.

7. Dr. William Ammon, *Walking Our Loved Ones Home* (Pen Argyl, Pennsylvania: Practical Christian Living Ministries, Inc., 1995), 78.

8. John F. Mac Arthur, Jr. and Wayne A. Mack, *Introduction to Biblical Counseling* (Nashville, Tennessee: W Publishing Group, 1994), 206.

9. Letitia Ann Peplar and Daniel Perlman, *Loneliness: A Sourcebook of Current Theory, Research, and Therapy* (New York, New York: Wiley-Interscience Publications, 1982), 3.

10. Leslie B. Flynn, *Gifts of the Spirit* (Wheaton, Illinois: Victor Books, 1974), 135.

11. Clark E. Moustabar, *Loneliness* (Detroit, Michigan: Prentice-Hall, Inc., 1961), 102.

12. Dean Turner, *Lonely God, Lonely Man* (New York, New York: Philosophical Library Inc., 1960), 157.

13. Samuel M. Natale, *Loneliness and Spiritual Growth* (Birmingham, Alabama: Religious Education Press, 1986), 156.

14. Dr. Frank B. Minerth, and Dr. Paul A. Meier, *Happiness is a Choice* (Grand Rapids, Michigan: Baker Book House, 1978), 144.

CHAPTER TWO: DISTURBED

1. *Webster's New World Dictionary* David B Guralnek, Editor in Chief (Cleveland, Ohio: William Collins Publishers, Inc., 1979), 1299.

2. Gene Edwards, *Exquisite Agony* (Jacksonville, Florida: The Seed Sowers, 1994), 13.

3. Dr. Eric P. Masse, *The Conquest of Loneliness* (New York, New York: Random House, 1957), 193.

4. Ida Nelle Hollaway, *Loneliness: The Untapped Resource* (Nashville, Tennessee: Broadman Press, 1982), 87.

5. Ibid., 107.

6. Maureen C. Tirabassi, "Loneliness is a Four Letter Word", *The Living Pulpit* Vol. 9, No 1 (January/March 2000): 5.

7. Edgar N. Jackson, *Theology* Vol. 84, No 701 (September, 1981): 387.

8. Ibid., 387.

9. Craig W. Ellison, "The Roots of Loneliness", *Christianity Today* (10 March 1978): 12,13.

10. Erwin R. McManus, *Soul Cravings* (Nashville, Tennessee: Nelson Books,2006), 4.

11. C.S. Lewis, *A Grief Observed* (San Francisco, California: Harper and Row Publishers, 1961), 9.

CHAPTER THREE: DESPERATE

1. "How to Handle Loneliness," *In Touch Ministries* available from http://www.intouch.org; 2/20/2007.

2. Lila Empson and Bryan Norman, eds., *The New Rebellion Handbook* (Brentwood, Tennessee: Nelson Books, 2006), 30.

3. Ibid., 30.

4. David Johnson and Jeff Van Vondersen, *The Subtle Power of Spiritual Abuse* (Minneapolis, Minnesota: Bethany House Publishers, 1991), 20.

5. Dr. Elizabeth Kübler-Ross, *On Death and Dying* (New York: Touchstone, 1969), 60.

6. Daniel Goleman, *Emotional Intelligence* (New York: Bantam Books, 1994), 268.

7. Randy Alcorn, *Heaven* (Wheaton, Illinois: Tyndale House Publishers, Inc., 2004), 327.

8. William E. Hulme, *Creative Loneliness* (Minneapolis, Minnesota: Augusburg Publishing House, 1977), 50.

CHAPTER FOUR: DOLDRUMS

1. Matthew Henry, *A Commentary of the Bible, Vol. III* (Aston Place, New York: Funk & Wagnells, 1820), 366.

2. Marshall Shelley, *Well-Intentioned Dragons* (Minneapolis, Minnesota: Bethany House Publishers, 1985), 79.

3. C.S. Lewis, *Problem of Pain* (New York: MacMillan Publishing Co., Inc., 1962), 99.

4. Greg Laurie, *The Best is Yet to Come* (Sisters, Oregon: Multnomah Publishers, 2005), 134,135.

5. George Barna, *Revolution* (Carol Stream, Illinois: Tyndale House Publisher, Inc., 2005), 89.

6. Ibid., 26.

7. Ron Mehl, *Surprise Endings* (Sisters, Oregon: Multnomah Publishers, 1993), 99.

8. *Webster's New World Dictionary* David B Guralnek, Editor in Chief (Cleveland, Ohio: William Collins Publishers, Inc., 1979), 559.

9. Ron Mehl, 106-109.

10. Louis Paul Lehman, *Tears of the Bible* (Grand Rapids, Michigan: Zondervan Publishing House, 1958), 78.

11. Marshall Shelley, 91.

12. C.S. Lewis, 98.

13. *Webster's New World Dictionary* David B Guralnek, Editor in Chief (Cleveland, Ohio: William Collins Publishers, Inc., 1979), 415.

14. Philip Yancey, *Disappointment with God* (Grand Rapids, Michigan: Zondervan Publishing House, 1988), 98,99.

15. Jerry Bridges, *Trusting God* (Colorado Springs, Colorado: Navpress, 1988), 177.

16. Charles R. Solomon, *The Ins and Outs of Rejection* (Sevierville, Tennessee: Solomon Publications, 1991), 202.

17. Martin and Deidre Bobgan, *12 Steps to Destruction* (Santa Barbara, California: East Gate Publishers, 1991), 17.

18. Francis A. Schaeffer, *He is There and He is Not Silent* (Wheaton, Illinois: Tyndale House Publishers, 1972), 18.

19. C.S. Lewis, *Mere Christianity* (New York: The MacMillan Company, 1956), 148.

20. Gerald L. Sittser, *A Grace Disguised* (Grand Rapids, Michigan: Zondervan Publishing House, 1995), 47.

CHAPTER FIVE: DEVOTED

1. Larry Crabb, *Shattered Dreams* (Colorado Springs, Colorado: Waterbrook Press, 2005), 67.

2. Walter B. Greenway, *Lenton Sermons* (Philadelphia, Pennsylvania: Harvey M. Shelley Publisher, 1927), 136.

3. Bill Bright, *The Journey Home* (Nashville, Tennessee: Thomas Nelson Publishers, 2003), 76.

4. Lynne Dugan, "Pastor's Wives," *Time,* 19 Apr. 2007, 48.

5. *News and Observer,* 3 Apr. 2007, p. 1. [quoting Shankar Vedentam, *The Washington Post*]

6. Ibid., 1.

7. Robert S. Weise, *Loneliness, The Experience of Emotional and Social Isolation* (Cambridge, Massachusetts: The MIT Press, 1973), 10.

8. Jean and Veryl Rosenbaum, *Conquering Loneliness* (New York: Hawthorne Books, Inc., 1973), 64.

9. Edgar N. Jackson, *Understanding Loneliness* (Philadelphia, Pennsylvania: Fortress Press, 1980), 132.

10. Mary Foxwell Loeks, *The Glorious Names of God* (Grand Rapids, Michigan: Baker Bookhouse, 1986), 84.

11. Gerald L. Sittser, *A Grace Disguised* (Grand Rapids, Michigan: Zondervan Publishing House, 1995), 60.

12. Dr. Dan B. Allender and Dr. Trenper Longman III, *The Cry of the Soul* (Colorado Springs, Colorado: Navpress, 1994), 31.

13. *Webster's New World Dictionary* David B Guralnek, Editor in Chief (Cleveland, Ohio: William Collins Publishers, Inc., 1979), 387.

14. R. Kent Hughes, *Disciplines of a Godly Man* (Wheaton, Illinois: Crossway Books, 1991), 111.

15. Ibid., 140.

16. Ibid.

17. Lila Empson and Bryan Norman, eds., *The New Rebellion Handbook* (Brentwood, Tennessee: Nelson Books, 2006), 121.

18. Ruth Graham Bell, "We Live a Time" Available from http://www.billygraham.org?RBG_Time To Adore.asp; Internet; accessed 12 July 2007.

EPILOGUE

1. *Webster's New World Dictionary* David B Guralnek, Editor in Chief (Cleveland, Ohio: William Collins Publishers, Inc., 1979), 1218.

2. Billy Graham, *The Holy Spirit* (Waco, Texas: Word Book Publishers, 1978), 192.

3. George Barna, *Revolution* (Carol Stream, Illinois: Tyndale House Publishers, Inc., 2005), 19.

BIBLIOGRAPHY

Alcorn, Randy. *Heaven.* Wheaton, Illinois: Tyndale House Publishers, 2004.

Allender, Dr. Dan B. and Dr. Trenper Longman III. *The Cry of the Soul.* Colorado Springs, Colorado: Navpress, 1994.

Ammon, Dr. William. *Walking Our Loved Ones Home.* Pen Argyl, Pennsylvania: Practical Christian Living Ministries, Inc., 1995.

Barna, George. *Revolution.* Carol Stream, Illinois: Tyndale House Publishers, Inc., 2005.

Bobgan, Martin and Deidre. *12 Steps to Destruction.* Santa Barbara, California: East Gate Publishers, 1991.

Bridges, Jerry. *Trusting God.* Colorado Springs, Colorado: Navpress, 1988.

Bright, Bill. *The Journey Home.* Nashville, Tennessee: Thomas Nelson Publishers, Inc., 2003.

Crabb, Larry. *Shattered Dreams*. Colorado Springs, Colorado: Waterbrook Press, 2005.

Dobson, Dr. James. *When God Doesn't Make Sense*. Wheaton, Illinois: Tyndale House Publishers, 1993.

Dugan, Lynne. "Pastor's Wives," *Time,* 19 Apr. 2007, 48.

Edwards, Gene. *Exquisite Agony.* Jacksonville, Florida: The Seed Sowers, 1994.

Eldridge, John. *Epic.* Nashville, Tennessee: Thomas Nelson, Inc., 2004.

Ellison, Craig W. "The Roots of Loneliness." *Christianity Today.* 10 March 1978, 12-16.

Empson, Lila, and Bryan Norman, eds. *The New Rebellion Handbook.* Brentwood, Tennessee: Nelson Books, 2006.

Facts and Trends Vol. 53, No. 2. March/April 2007.

Flynn, Leslie B. *Gifts of the Spirit.* Wheaton, Illinois: Victor Books, 1974.

Goleman, Daniel. *Emotional Intelligence.* New York: Bantam Books, 1994.

Graham, Billy. *The Holy Spirit.* Waco, Texas: Word Book Publisher, 1978.

Graham, Ruth Bell. "We Live a Time". Available from http://www.billygraham.org/RBG_TimeToAdore.asp, Internet. Accessed 12 July 2007.

Greenway, Walter B. *Lenton Sermons.* Philadelphia, Pennsylvania: Harvey M. Publisher, 1927.

Henry, Matthew. *A Commentary on the Bible, Vol. III.* Aston Place, New York: Funk and Wagnells, 1820.

Hollaway, Ida Nelle. *Loneliness: The Untapped Resource.* Nashville Tennessee: Broadman Press, 1982.

"How to Handle Loneliness," *In Touch Ministries.* 20 February 2007. article on line. available from http//www.intouch.org. accessed 15 March 2007.

Hughes, R. Kent. *Disciplines of a Godly Man.* Wheaton, Illinois: Crossway Books, 1991.

Hulme, William E. *Creative Loneliness.* Minneapolis, Minnesota: Augusburg Publishing House, 1977.

Jackson, Edgar N. *Theology.* Vol.84, No.701. September, 1981.

Jackson, Edgar N. *Understanding Loneliness.* Philadelphia, Pennsylvania: Fortress Press, 1980.

Johnson, David and Jeff Van Vonderson. *The Subtle Power of Spiritual Abuse.* Minneapolis, Minnesota: Bethany House Publishers, 1991.

Kübler-Ross, Dr. Elizabeth. *On Death and Dying.* New York: Touchstone, 1969.

Laurie, Greg. *The Best is Yet to Come.* Sisters, Oregon: Multnomah Publishers, 2005.

Lehman, Louis Paul. *Tears of the Bible.* Grand Rapids, Michigan: Zondervan Publishing House, 1958.

Lester, Andrew D. *It Hurts So Bad, Lord!* Nashville, Tennessee: Broadman Press, 1976.

Lewis, C.S. *A Grief Observed.* San Francisco, California: Harper and Row Publishers, 1961.

Lewis, C.S. *Mere Christianity.* New York: The MacMillan Company, 1956.

Lewis, C.S. *Problem of Pain.* New York: MacMillan Publishing Co., Inc., 1962.

Loeks, Mary Foxwell. *The Glorious Names of God.* Grand Rapids, Michigan: Baker Bookhouse, 1986.

Lucado, Max. *On the Anvil.* Wheaton, Illinois: Tyndale House Publishers, 1985.

Mac Arthur, John F. Jr., and Wayne A. Mack. *Introduction to Biblical Counseling.* Nashville, Tennessee: W Publishing Group, 1994.

Masse, Dr. Eric P. *The Conquest of Loneliness.* New York: Random House, 1957.

McManus, Erwin R. *Soul Cravings.* Nashville, Tennessee: Nelson Books, 2006.

Mehl, Ron. *Surprise Endings.* Sisters, Oregon: Multnomah Publishers, 1993.

Minerth, Dr. Frank B., and Dr. Paul A. Meier. *Happiness is a Choice.* Grand Rapids, Michigan: Baker Book House, 1978.

Moustabar, Clark E. *Loneliness.* Detroit, Michigan: Prentice-Hall, Inc., 1961.

Natale, Samuel M. *Loneliness and Spiritual Growth.* Birmingham, Alabama: Religious Education Press, 1986.

News and Observer, 3 Apr. 2007, 1.

Peplar, Letitia Ann and Daniel Perlman. *Loneliness: A Sourcebook of Current*

Theory, Research and Therapy. New York: Wiley-Interscience Publications, 1982.

Rosenbaum, Jean and Veryl. *Conquering Loneliness.* New York: Hawthorne Books, Inc., 1973.

Schaeffer, Francis A. *He is There and He is Not Silent.* Wheaton, Illinois: Tyndale House Publishers, 1972.

Shelley, Marshall. *Well-Intentioned Dragons.* Minneapolis, Minnesota: Bethany House Publishers, 1985.

Sittser, Gerald L. *A Grace Disguised.* Grand Rapids, Michigan: Zondervan Publishing House, 1995.

Solomon, Charles R. *The Ins and Outs of Rejection.* Sevierville, Tennessee: Solomon Publications, 1991.

Tirabassi, Maureen C. "Loneliness is a Four Letter Word," *The Living Pulpit.* Vol. 9, No.1. January/March, 2005, 4,5.

Turner, Dean. *Lonely God, Lonely Man.* New York: Philosophical Library Inc., 1960.

Westberg, Granger E. *Good Grief.* Philadelphia: Fortress Press, 1962.

Weise, Robert S. *Loneliness, The Experience of Emotional and Social Isolation.* Cambridge, Massachusetts: The MIT Press, 1973.

Wilkerson, David. *Suicide.* Lindale, Texas: David Wilkerson Publications, 1978.

Yancey, Philip. *Disappointment With God.* Grand Rapids, Michigan: Zondervan Publishing House, 1988.

About the Author

Peter H. Burgess was born and raised in North Carolina. He married Eunice Moore Burgess in 1952. Together they have three daughters, five grandchildren and two great grand sons.

Dr. Burgess earned his Bachelor of Arts degree at Bob Jones University. He acquired his Bachelor of Divinity and Master of Divinity degrees as a student at Northern Baptist Theological Seminary and the Doctor of Ministry and Doctor of Philosophy (c) at Trinity Theological Seminary.

Dr. Burgess has pastored congregations along the east coast, from New York to North Carolina. He has also served as a Bible teacher, Biblical counselor and seminary professor and has established the website: http://www.causewaycommunity.com.

Printed in the United States
129083LV00002B/145/P